THE BBC TV SHAKESPEARE
Literary Consultant: John Wilders

TITUS ANDRONICUS

THE BBC TV SHAKESPEARE

ALL'S WELL THAT ENDS WELL
ANTONY AND CLEOPATRA
AS YOU LIKE IT
THE COMEDY OF ERRORS
CORIOLANUS
CYMBELINE
HAMLET
HENRY IV Part 1
HENRY IV Part 2
HENRY V
HENRY VI Part 1
HENRY VI Part 2
HENRY VI Part 3
HENRY VIII
JULIUS CAESAR
KING JOHN
KING LEAR
LOVE'S LABOUR'S LOST
MACBETH
MEASURE FOR MEASURE
THE MERCHANT OF VENICE
THE MERRY WIVES OF WINDSOR
A MIDSUMMER NIGHT'S DREAM
MUCH ADO ABOUT NOTHING
OTHELLO
PERICLES
RICHARD II
RICHARD III
ROMEO AND JULIET
THE TAMING OF THE SHREW
THE TEMPEST
TIMON OF ATHENS
TITUS ANDRONICUS
TROILUS AND CRESSIDA
TWELFTH NIGHT
THE TWO GENTLEMEN OF VERONA
THE WINTER'S TALE

THE BBC TV SHAKESPEARE

Literary Consultant: John Wilders
Fellow of Worcester College, Oxford

Titus Andronicus

BRITISH BROADCASTING CORPORATION

Published by the
British Broadcasting Corporation
35 Marylebone High Street
London WIM 4AA

ISBN 0 563 20279 3

This edition first published 1986
© The British Broadcasting Corporation
and the Contributors 1986

The text of the Works of Shakespeare
edited by Peter Alexander
© William Collins Sons and Company Ltd 1951

The text of *Titus Andronicus* used in this volume is the Alexander text, edited by
the late Professor Alexander and chosen by the BBC as the basis for its
television production, and is reprinted by arrangement with William
Collins Sons and Company Ltd. The complete Alexander text is published
in one volume by William Collins Sons and Company Ltd under the title
The Alexander Text of the Complete Works of William Shakespeare.

All photographs are copyright BBC Enterprises Ltd

Printed in Great Britain at
The Bath Press, Avon

CONTENTS

PREFACE

John Wilders

Titus Andronicus was much more popular in Shakespeare's own time than it has been in our own. One indication of its popularity is that it was published three times while the dramatist was still alive, in 1594, 1600 and 1611. All three editions were quarto volumes of that single play, and the compositor used a copy of the First Quarto to set up the Second and a copy of the Second to set up the Third. Then when in 1623 the first collected edition of Shakespeare's plays, the First Folio, was produced, the printer used a copy of the Third Quarto as a basis for his text. Since fresh errors were introduced whenever the type was reset, the most reliable text, the closest to Shakespeare's original manuscript, is the First Quarto of 1594. In February of that year the play was entered in the Register of the Stationers' Company, a procedure which established the exclusive right of a particular printer, in this case John Danter, to publish it.

It was also in 1594 that a troupe of actors, the Earl of Sussex's men, put on the first recorded performance of *Titus Andronicus*. The play appears actually to have been written a few years earlier, however, for it is described on the title-page of the First Quarto as having already been performed by 'the Right Honourable the Earle of Darbie, Earle of Pembroke, and Earle of Sussex their Servants'. When precisely Shakespeare wrote it we do not know but the style in which it was written suggests that it was in 1592–93 – in other words, after he had completed the three parts of *Henry VI* and at about the time when he composed *The Comedy of Errors*. Some people have thought that it was not written entirely by Shakespeare, a theory first put forward by the dramatist Edward Ravenscroft who, in 1686, argued that it was the work of an inferior playwright to which Shakespeare added only 'some master touches to one or two of the principal parts of characters'. Although some more recent scholars have believed that it was written in collaboration with one or more other playwrights, the general belief nowadays is that it was the work of Shakespeare alone.

Unlike Shakespeare's other Roman plays, *Julius Caesar, Antony and Cleopatra* and *Coriolanus*, *Titus Andronicus* was not based on the historical biographies written by Plutarch, nor does it depict authentic historical events. Shakespeare may have taken his material from a prose work, *The History of Titus Andronicus*, *The Renowned Roman General*, of which no copy of the original edition has survived but which does exist in an eighteenth-century reprint. He was certainly much influenced by the Roman poet Ovid whose work he knew well and who, in his *Metamorphoses*, tells the story of Philomela who, like Lavinia in Shakespeare's play, is raped and has her tongue cut out to prevent her from telling her story.

Titus Andronicus appears to have been very popular in the Elizabethan and Jacobean theatre and, according to a remark made by Ben Jonson, was still well known twenty years after its first performance. Like many of Shakespeare's plays it was radically altered after the Restoration, this time by Edward Ravenscroft whose version, retitled *Titus Andronicus or The Rape of Lavinia*, was probably put on for the first time in 1678, though it was not published until nine years later. No further performances have been recorded before 1839 when an adaptation by a certain N. H. Bannister was given in Philadelphia. It was put on in London in 1852 with the celebrated black actor Ira Aldridge, 'the African Roscius', in the role of Aaron; the text he used, however, had been even more drastically altered than Ravenscroft's. Shakespeare's original play was not brought back to the stage before 1923 when Robert Atkins directed it at the Old Vic. The most memorable production in the twentieth century, and possibly the greatest in the play's history, was directed by Peter Brook at Stratford-on-Avon in 1955 with Laurence Olivier as Titus, Vivien Leigh as Lavinia and Anthony Quayle as Aaron. A shortened version was put on at the Old Vic in 1957 under the direction of Walter Hudd with Derek Godfrey as Titus, Keith Michell as Aaron and Barbara Jefford as Tamora, and in Trevor Nunn's production at Stratford in 1972 Colin Blakely was Titus, Janet Suzman Lavinia and John Wood Saturninus.

This production by Jane Howell was recorded at the BBC Television Centre in February 1985.

8

INTRODUCTION TO
TITUS ANDRONICUS

John Wilders

When we talk about Shakespeare's 'Roman plays' we are usually thinking of his three great tragedies *Julius Caesar*, *Antony and Cleopatra* and *Coriolanus*. Very early in his career, however, Shakespeare wrote another Roman play, *Titus Andronicus*, which, though immensely popular in his own time, is nowadays seldom read and rarely performed. *Titus* has been neglected because it has been considered too crudely violent and sensational, an Elizabethan horror play written in the manner of another well-tried favourite with Shakespeare's audiences, Thomas Kyd's *The Spanish Tragedy*, and, in its excessive brutality, significant only as an example of a popular taste which Shakespeare rapidly outgrew as he improved in skill, subtlety and discrimination. The man who revised the play shortly after the Restoration, Edward Ravenscroft, described it as 'a heap of rubbish' and, though subsequent critics have chosen their words more carefully, most of them have agreed with his judgment.

It has recently been realised, however, that Shakespeare took more trouble in the writing of this early tragedy than had been generally assumed. With its abundance of references to Roman history, legend and literature, it is a play designed for the learned as well as the vulgar playgoer. Moreover, as in his later Roman tragedies, Shakespeare took the trouble to give it what was, for him, a characteristically Roman flavour, to create the impression of a society very different from his own, with distinctive ideals, institutions, and habits of mind and life. The historical period portrayed in *Titus Andronicus* is not the same as that depicted in *Julius Caesar* and *Antony and Cleopatra*, a period in which Rome was still a republic at the peak of its military power and about which Shakespeare read in the biographies of the historian Plutarch. The Rome in which *Titus Andronicus* is set is the imperial Rome of several centuries later, notorious for its corruption and the depravity of its emperors, and assailed by its lawless enemies the Goths, the northern tribes who eventually destroyed it. The sexual excesses and physical violence which play an important part in the action of the tragedy, such as the rape and mutilation of Lavinia, the execution of Titus' sons and Tamora's infatuation with Aaron the Moor, were derived by Shakespeare not so much from earlier tragedies of blood but from such knowledge of late imperial Roman history as he acquired from reading Suetonius, or at any rate the sixteenth-century historians who took their material from him. 'When the Roman Empire were grown to its height', began one such writer,

> and the greatest part of the world was subjected to its imperial throne, in the time of Theodosius, a barbarous northern people out of Swedeland, Denmark and Gothland came into Italy in such numbers under the leading of Tottilius, their King, that they overran it with fire and sword, plundering churches, ripping up women with child, and deflowering virgins in so horrid and barbarous a manner that the people fled before them like flocks of sheep.

These are the opening words of *The History of Titus Andronicus*, a little book which some scholars believe was the principal source of the play. It certainly creates a strong impression of the world of the tragedy itself.

There was, moreover, a dramatist with whose work Shakespeare was very familiar, the Latin playwright Seneca, whose works were studied assiduously by Elizabethan schoolboys and whose tragedies, already translated into English by 1581, depicted brutally sensational deeds similar to those in *Titus Andronicus* – adultery, incest, unnatural murder and, above all, revenge. The kind of events portrayed in them correspond quite closely to those recorded by the historians of late imperial Rome, and in writing this, his most Senecan tragedy, Shakespeare may not simply have been imitating a well-known Latin model but attempting to give what he believed to be a realistic impression of Roman life at that time. In other words he imitated Seneca in order to create an impression of historical authenticity.

This is certainly the motive behind the Latin quotations which crop up frequently in the dialogue. On discovering that it is the sons of Tamora who have deflowered his daughter, Titus exclaims,

> Magni Dominator poli,
> Tam lentus audis scelera? tam lentus vides?

('Ruler of the great heavens, dost thou so calmly hear crimes, so calmly look on them?') He is quoting from Seneca's tragedy *Hippo-*

lytus and, in response, he sends a bundle of weapons to the two rapists together with a scroll on which are written some lines of Latin verse which one of them identifies as a quotation from Horace. Elsewhere there are references to Roman heroes such as Coriolanus and Aeneas and to Latin mythology and literature, particularly Ovid's *Metamorphoses*, a copy of which Lavinia points to:

> Soft! So busily she turns the leaves! Help her.
> What would she find? Lavinia, shall I read?
> This is the tragic tale of Philomel
> And treats of Tereus' treason and his rape.

'The tragic tale of Philomel' as told by Ovid (another author much studied in Elizabethan schools) was also a major source of Shakespeare's play, for Philomel was raped by her own brother-in-law, King Tereus of Thrace, in 'a hut deep hidden in the ancient woods', and, in order to prevent her from revealing his guilt, Tereus cut out her tongue. As they watched the first performances of *Titus Andronicus*, Shakespeare's contemporaries, unlike our own, could scarcely have failed to recognise that they were being shown a recognisably Roman drama, full of references to a literature with which many of them were extremely familiar. At times, indeed, he goes so far as to imitate Ovid's characteristically vivid metaphorical style, as in Marcus' description of Lavinia's bleeding mouth:

> Why dost not speak to me?
> Alas, a crimson river of warm blood,
> Like to a bubbling fountain stirr'd with wind,
> Doth rise and fall between thy rosed lips,
> Coming and going with thy honey breath.

It has recently been pointed out that this passage is quite close in style to Ovid's account of the death of Pyramus (which Shakespeare was to turn to farce several years later in *A Midsummer Night's Dream*):

> As he lay stretched upon the earth the spouting blood leaped high; just as when a pipe has broken at a weak spot in the lead and through the small hissing aperture sends spurting forth long streams of water, cleaving the air with its jets.

It is clear, then, that Shakespeare took particular care to give to his play a recognisably authentic Roman colouring. This is important because its major preoccupation is one which was extremely pertinent to Rome at the very point in its history with which it deals. Rome is portrayed at a point of crisis, poised between the stability which had been supported by the patriotism, religious faith and moral principles of the past and the anarchic violence displayed by its enemies the Goths, and now, more dangerously, erupting from within Rome itself. In this struggle, Gothic brutality is shown in the ruthless, lustful Empress Tamora, her vicious sons and her Moorish lover, and Roman integrity is centred in the opposing family, that of Titus and his children who have devoted, and in some cases sacrificed, their lives to their country.

Titus himself is that not uncommon Shakespearian character, the survivor from an earlier and more honourable age, like Kent in *King Lear*, Gloucester in *Henry VI* and Adam the old servant in *As You Like It*, shocked and bewildered by the cunning self-interested deceivers with whom he is compelled to associate. He is distinguished principally by his military achievements, and is referred to from the outset as

>   The good Andronicus,
>   Patron of virtue, Rome's best champion,
>   Successful in the battles that he fights,

who

>   With honour and with fortune is return'd
>   From where he circumscribed with his sword
>   And brought to yoke the enemies of Rome.

The first emotion he expresses is of love for his country for which, already, twenty of his sons have given up their lives, and whose soil he greets with 'tears of true joy'. He also displays another characteristically Roman virtue, the love of his family. He addresses his daughter Lavinia as 'the cordial of mine age to glad my heart', and his first actions are to give decent burial to his most recently killed sons and, in accordance with religious custom, to sacrifice one of the captured enemy in order that their souls may rest in peace. The ceremony of burial at which he officiates in the first scene links him firmly with traditional religious beliefs and family piety:

>   In peace and honour rest you here, my sons;
>   Rome's readiest champions, repose you here in rest,
>   Secure from worldly chances and mishaps!
>   Here lurks no treason, here no envy swells,
>   Here grow no damned drugs, here are no storms,
>   No noise, but silence and eternal sleep.
>   In peace and honour rest you here, my sons!

In the respect they are anxious to pay to their dead brothers and in the patriotism and courage they have already shown, Titus' children clearly act on convictions similar to their father's. His refusal to accede to the wishes of the people and stand as a candidate for the imperial throne is consistent with the self-denial he has already displayed in battle, and in this he resembles one of Shakespeare's later Roman heroes, Coriolanus.

The opening scene of *Titus Andronicus*, with its public orations, funeral procession, ceremony of interment and the acclamation of Saturninus as Emperor, is extremely formal and ritualistic, creating the impression that ancient, traditional rites are being decently observed. These ceremonies, however, are seldom carried to their conclusions but are interrupted by sudden outbursts of violence, as when the new Emperor's brother carries off his prospective bride, Titus rashly kills his son Mutius, and the two brothers Saturninus and Bassianus openly defy each other. These eruptions are a foretaste of the worse horrors to come, and, in the threats they make to the proper performance of traditional ceremonies, are a representation of the conflict which develops as the play unfolds, a conflict between social and familial order and the anarchy which results when the loyalties which bind societies together are broken. The abduction of Lavinia and the subsequent marriage of the Emperor to the Queen of the Goths are the first steps towards the 'wilderness of tigers' into which the city degenerates. The observation of ceremony and the mutual respect which such ceremonies as burial, marriage and coronation express are one of the ways in which, according to the terms set up in this play, societies are restrained from following the law of the jungle.

The first offender against these obligations is the new Emperor himself who, having publicly pledged himself to marry Lavinia, the daughter of the victorious general, is then led by his sexual appetite to choose Tamora, an enemy queen, as his bride and to marry her with indecent haste. Thus placed in a position of authority, Tamora uses her power not, as Titus had done, for the good of Rome, but in order to gratify her desire for revenge on Titus and his family, which now becomes the motivating force behind the tragedy:

> I'll find a day to massacre them all,
> And raze their faction and their family,
> The cruel father and his traitorous sons,
> To whom I sued for my dear son's life.

In the brutality which she both practises and encourages, Tamora becomes the most vicious of the 'tigers' which take over the city.

The outrages which are subsequently committed – the murder of Bassianus, the rape and dismemberment of Lavinia, the unjust execution of Titus' remaining sons – are carried out by Chiron and Demetrius, abetted by their barbaric mother, ostensibly as acts of vengeance for their defeat at the hands of Titus and the latter's sacrifice of their brother. But it is also clear that they take pleasure in causing pain and grief to others. The mutilation of Lavinia is made to seem unnatural not simply because she is innocent and helpless but because it is carried out in a naturally beneficent setting when 'the morn is bright and grey, The fields are fragrant, and the woods are green'. The 'wide and spacious' forest walks are seen by the lascivious brothers merely as 'unfrequented plots . . . Fitted by kind for rape and villainy'. For Tamora, too, the song of the birds and the 'green leaves quivering with the cooling wind' provide an apt setting for unnatural and adulterous lust. Unnaturalness is, throughout the play, the distinguishing feature of the Empress and her sons. It is she who encourages them to assault Lavinia while she is satisfying her appetite on the Moor. In his revenge on her, Titus induces her, unwittingly, to commit the most unnatural act of all, to eat a pie made from the flesh of her own children.

A similar delight in villainy is shown by her lover, Aaron the Moor, whom Shakespeare introduces into the play with some dramatic subtlety and power. Aaron is first brought on by the victorious Titus together with his other prisoners and, the only black figure on a stage otherwise occupied by white characters, he quickly makes a strong impression. As the long opening scene unfolds, moreover, he gradually becomes more noticeable as the only major character to remain silent. He says nothing until at the very end of the scene he is left alone, and at that point he delivers his first long soliloquy, and thereby satisfies the curiosity he has, by this time, aroused. The solitariness of Aaron suits him well, for he is an alien who, unlike the other major characters, has no family and no loyalties to prevent him from furthering his own desires, and it soon becomes clear that he intends to exploit the weaknesses of others for his own ends:

> Then Aaron, arm thy heart and fit thy thoughts
> To mount aloft with thy imperial mistress,
> And mount her pitch whom thou in triumph long
> Hast prisoner held, fett'red in amorous chains,
> And faster bound to Aaron's charming eyes
> Than is Prometheus tied to Caucasus.

Aaron is the forerunner of a number of unscrupulous adventurers who make their appearance in Shakespeare's later plays, such as Edmund in *King Lear* and Iachimo in *Cymbeline*. Like the sons of Tamora he is eager to satisfy his sexual appetites without scruple, but unlike them he is cunningly intelligent, teaching them how to annoy Lavinia without being discovered, and, later, how to conceal the child which he has himself fathered on the Empress. Like his associates, he openly delights in causing pain, but they need his perverse ingenuity to help them to carry out their misdeeds:

Even now I curse the day – and yet, I think,
Few come within the compass of my curse –
Wherein I did not some notorious ill:
As kill a man, or else devise his death;
Ravish a maid, or plot the way to do it;
Accuse some innocent, and forswear myself;
Set deadly enmity between two friends;
Make poor men's cattle break their necks;
Set fire on barns and hay-stacks in the night,
And bid the owners quench them with their tears.
Oft have I digg'd up dead men from their graves,
And set them upright at their dear friends' door
Even when their sorrows almost was forgot.

Aaron is, at any rate in this speech, so unhesitatingly villainous as to be scarcely credible though, like Richard III, he has in his frankness and vitality a certain bracing charm. But he is also an example of the kind of brutality which Tamora and her sons have brought into the gates of Rome. Unexpectedly, however, he does ultimately reveal a humanity of which his associates are incapable, in his love and concern for his bastard child.

It would, however, be a distortion of the play to see it simply as a struggle between Roman honour and Gothic savagery. A degeneration also takes place within the Romans themselves, in Saturninus by his marriage to Tamora, in Titus by his rejection of Tamora's plea for her son's life, by his impetuous killing of his son Mutius, and, most of all, in the monstrous revenge which he inflicts on his enemies as the play concludes. The tiger lurks within Rome as well as outside it. For most of the play, however, Titus arouses our sympathy as he endures one outrage after another. Though the actual events depicted in the tragedy are violently sensational, Shakespeare's expression of the feelings they arouse is not. He gives moving expression to emotions which in real life might be felt but could not be articulated, and the play is full of the poetry of grief:

> For now I stand as one upon a rock,
> Environ'd with a wilderness of sea,
> Who marks the waxing tide grow wave by wave,
> Expecting ever when some envious surge
> Will in his brinish bowels swallow him.

Whereas his enemies are impervious to human feeling, and, indeed, enjoy the spectacle of others' sufferings, Titus, in his desolation, gives voice to those natural sympathies and convictions which have been violated: loyalty to his country, paternal love and especially justice as when, in his frenzy, he sends arrows up to the gods, bearing the message (also taken from Ovid) 'Terras Astraea reliquit', 'Justice has left the earth'.

In his impassioned protests against the wrongs inflicted on him, and in his desperate appeals for justice, Titus prefigures King Lear but, unlike Lear, he never matures into an acceptance of his sufferings. On the contrary, his grief converts to hatred and, in the act of vengeance with which he repays his enemies, he sinks to their level. As in the three parts of *Henry VI* which he had written only a year or two earlier, Shakespeare shows that violence provokes violence and that revenge breeds further revenges which cease only when all the perpetrators have been destroyed. Hence it is right that Titus should himself be killed and that not he but his son Lucius should take on the government of Rome. It is only then, as Titus' brother Marcus declares, that the Roman people, hitherto at war with one another, can unite:

> You sad-fac'd men, people and sons of Rome,
> By uproars sever'd, as a flight of fowl
> Scatter'd by winds and high tempestuous gusts,
> O, let me teach you how to knit again
> This scattered corn into one mutual sheaf,
> These broken limbs again into one body;
> Lest Rome herself be bane unto herself,
> And she whom mighty kingdoms curtsy to,
> Like a forlorn and desperate castaway,
> Do shameful execution on herself.

The play concludes, as it began, with preparations for the rites of burial, and this reference to the traditional proprieties suggests that the city has returned to its former stability.

THE PRODUCTION

Henry Fenwick

Titus Andronicus is a play of such horrifying bloodiness, such gruesome grotesquerie, that, since its first enormous popularity with
Shakespeare's own audiences, it has largely been dismissed as an
early, crude work, one or two good things in it, but not worthy of
much consideration except for its being by Shakespeare. An
elderly, ruthless Roman hero, returning to Rome in triumph, is
repaid by having his conquered enemy made Empress and his
family decimated, by rape, mutilation and murder, until he finally
attains revenge in a repulsively primitive manner, by feeding the
flesh of her dead sons to the Empress in a pie. On the way to this
climax he goes through several changes, and at one point, appar-
ently mad, reproaches his brother for killing a fly.

'It was the scene with the fly, really, that got me,' says the director, Jane Howell, 'and realising there was a boy [Titus' grandson,
Young Lucius] watching all these horrors. Up until that point I'd
found it rather farcical. That's what focused my imagination: I
thought the scene was very beautiful and very important: "How if
that fly had a father and mother?" seemed a key and crucial line.
I thought it was an extraordinary scene and became convinced
that Shakespeare and nobody else had written that scene, and
that's really why I took the play on. You need a lynchpin; for a
play as difficult as this one you need to find a way into it for
yourself.'

We were talking as she was editing the opening shots, a beautiful
mix of smoke from the sacrificial fires of the first scene, skulls
carried on poles, and the intelligent, startled face of Paul Davies-
Prowles, the young actor playing the boy, Young Lucius. 'Once I'd
cottoned on to the boy,' she said, 'and thought about putting him at
the beginning and end of the play and seeing it through his eyes, it
seemed to me to make things possible. The play has some strange
logical shifts – well, not *logical* shifts, but characters seem to change
very rapidly, especially in that very big scene with Saturninus and
Bassianus, the election. Once I got on to the boy I thought, "Oh, I

see, it has the logic of a dream, which is fairly consistent but has some odd things in it."''

Deciding to give the production the atmosphere of a boy's dream/nightmare immediately affected all the aspects of design in the production. Nothing needed to be too strictly 'Roman'. 'I never thought of it as the Rome of steps and white pillars,' Jane says, and Tony Burrough's set creates a Coliseum-like circle of rough, crumbling stones, crude stairs and arches, tunnel-like exits. Texture, he says, was one of the things he concentrated on. Jane and he consulted a book on walls – their texture, their degrees of decay – in pursuit of the proper look of decadent strength. It is not the look we traditionally think of as classical, but rather barbaric, uncouth. The costumes, too, are unclassical in feeling. 'It's a medieval rather than a correct Roman costume,' says costume designer Colin Lavers. 'It's imaginary – as though the boy has read some horrific story of the worst excesses of the Roman Empire and then had a nightmare. The only thing Roman is the armour, which had to be hired, so you're locked into what you can hire. We just made it as plain as possible. So the Romans were in brown leather and the Goths in suede and studs.

'With any period production, you know, you can always say, "That was made in the sixties" or "That was made in the seventies." No matter if it's a period production, you're always influenced by the styles of the times you're working in. This is an eighties' production. The Goths were influenced by a pop group called Kiss – heavy boots and breeches and chains: eighties' barbarism. Long hair and lots of studs and painted faces – modern barbarians. Nothing is strict research on my part: it's based on this idea of the boy dreaming. Anything I knew about Rome I kept in the back of my head while doing it, trying for the essence of Rome, but in no way correct. I don't like purple so the only person in purple is the Emperor and after that it's lilacs and lavenders. Tamora being a warrior queen, it seemed a good opportunity to turn her into an Amazon.' In fact Tamora is decked in an assortment of eyecatching, chunky jewellery, as though she was carrying the exchequer on her arms and neck – an enormous necklet is based (eighties' influence again) on a photograph from a fashion magazine that Colin has had filed for five years – a photograph which he liked and kept, as most designers do, magpie-like, with bits and pieces that take their fancy, for the time when it might come in useful.

'The biggest problem,' he points out, 'was what to do about the hands!' To be exact, what he is talking about is the presence or absence of hands – both Lavinia and Titus lose those appendages during the action of the play, and make-up designer Cécile Hay-Arthur, queen of gore ever since *Richard III*, has created some rather effective stumps. Nevertheless, even in the pursuit of verisimilitude actors Trevor Peacock and Anna Calder-Marshall didn't go so far as to lose their own, and this fact it was Colin's problem to disguise. 'The only way I could think of was to try to break up the proportion of the arm with long, very loose-fitting sleeves, trying to disguise the length from shoulder to elbow and elbow to wrist. And that sort of sleeve can't be restricted to Lavinia and Titus or the moment they walk on you know they're the ones who are going to lose their hands. You've got to spread it around a bit.'

One of the most striking details of the production's design is the fact that the extras – soldiers, tribunes – wear masks. It's an idea, Jane Howell explains, that began in her mind with the principals and then moved from them on to the supernumeraries. 'I found it very peculiar,' she says, 'the way the characters changed so rapidly, and when I read the play first I had the sort of image that people had masks on and they kept changing their masks as they seemed to be contradicting the way they were the moment before. Then I got on to the boy, but the idea of the masks stayed with me and got transferred on to the extras. Unlike most crowds in Shakespeare, for whom you can find a reason for their being there – they have a purpose, a function – these seemed to have no function at all, and it's very horrid for people to stand around with nothing to do. And because they have no lines, and also because the play is so strange, I didn't know what to tell them to do, really, I didn't know how to tell them to react. They just seemed to have blank faces all the time, to me, just staring at these events almost like passive on-lookers. So it seemed to me that they could serve a function better in a way by just representing Rome, the tribunes, the ruling class of Rome. So the idea of masks, which I'd first felt about the main characters, got transferred to them and I thought it gave them a dignity. That's how the masks came about.'

'It is one of the earliest plays,' stresses producer Shaun Sutton. 'It is an unashamed, full-blooded revenge tragedy, cruel, gruesome, piling horror on horror. It was very popular with the Elizabethans, who obviously enjoyed not only the physical cruelties and mutil-ations – arms and legs being cut off must have given them a great kick – but they must also have liked the incredible viciousness and deviousness. And the grotesqueness – going off with a man's hand between your teeth – dear God, it's on the edge of a laugh, isn't it?

'I've always thought of it as a nonsense play, and it's been dismissed through the centuries, but this production convinced me that there's a hell of a good play there. It does seem to be a very seriously written and a very firmly constructed one, full of the promise of better things to come. The quality of the verse is very varied but there are fine passages, and the more you read it the more you realise it. Shakespeare has yet to learn his marvellous gift for dialogue – people are often talking in monologues, not picking up on what the other chap says, the characters tend to orate rather than talk to each other. But the character of Titus is interesting – in the way he changes, becomes wily, and particularly in the matter of his madness – how much is simulated, how much is real. There's a touch of the Hamlets there. We know the play has immaturities but they're not immaturities of construction, they're immaturities of character and character development. There is a very firm hand on the construction of the play, and a very serious force of writing that must have foretold, to the Elizabethans, the coming of a great playwright.'

The television production of *Titus* was unique in this cycle in that it was actually rehearsed and readied for production twice: the first time they were all set to begin shooting when a strike intervened. So enthusiastic had director and producer become over what had happened in the first rehearsal period that they insisted on gathering the same cast together as far as was possible, even though the logistics of such a remount meant a year went by before the show was at last in front of the cameras. For most of the actors this turned out to be an enormous blessing. 'The best thing in the world,' said Eileen Atkins, playing the wicked empress Tamora, 'was to rehearse it at that intensity and then leave it for a year. I swear nobody thought they were thinking about it but it was at the back of the mind all the time: "You know you may have to do *Titus* again." So it's sort of sitting there germinating and everybody came back with a totally different feeling. I loathed the play last year: I kept thinking "Oh, dear!" But as soon as we came back, within two days, I was utterly fascinated by it. We all liked it better; I suppose it became more cathartic this year and not just frightening. I don't know exactly why.'

The vengeful Tamora, whose son is sacrificed by Titus in the first scene and whose main mission in life thereafter becomes to destroy him and his family, is a figure of much-larger-than-life bloody-mindedness. 'I think,' says Ms Atkins, 'the crucial thing as far as I'm concerned is her utter misery and fury at her son's death. I think she just did not expect it – she thought the war was over and she went crazy with fury when Titus did that. It was bad enough being taken prisoner but then these bloody Romans with their wretched sacrifices that the Goths didn't have in that way – my line to him is "O cruel, irreligious piety" – I think she understood revenge, hatred, violent killings, even killing for fun, but to do it for this sacrificial rubbish drove her potty.'

She takes the cruelty of the play with a practical matter-of-factness, which she admits is probably easier because she is playing a baddy. 'The first night of *Titus*, when it was actually first played, there were seven heads on poles on the way to the theatre. So it's awfully silly of us to keep being so squeamish. We have our own miseries today. I like Tamora now. She likes running things and she'd probably run them quite well in Gothland. I've made myself think the Romans are so boring they deserve everything they get. Obviously Gothland has a lot more going for it. I was reading a history of the time and the Romans were endlessly going in there and pillaging and raping and God knows what, and they were sick to death of the Romans doing it – they weren't the aggressors. I was very keen on her looking foreign and not anything like anyone in Rome – I thought of trying an accent but you can't really do a big part in Shakespeare in an accent. Even if I looked bizarre I didn't care, I wanted no ordinariness about her at all. So if nothing else they're stunned by her differentness – it's very attractive, the alien.'

There cannot, of course, be anything in anybody's everyday life today to compare with Tamora's experiences, so what, I asked her, did she draw on? 'Imagination!' she says. 'I don't even have children – of course I can imagine but I don't have the true experience. I did one day wonder "What would you feel like if someone said you'd just eaten your three cats in that pie" – but giving yourself a real thing isn't nearly as good as imagining it. And you've got to imagine yourself in period – *then*. I loved it as soon as we got in the studio and the braziers started going – I really got quite scared when I was brought in as the prisoner. Every actor has different methods.'

She is sure, though, that the play works better for her on television. She compares it with her classic performance as *The Duchess of Malfi*, which is in the BBC archives. 'I think there is a slight pull back in you as an actress if you know you're going to have things like chopped hands. On stage you know that the audience knows that it's waxworks and there's a slight inhibiting thing: "I've got to make you believe". When you do it on the television there's the ability to be nearer to reality. And on stage if you're terrified that people are going to laugh you don't play out as full as you might, you can't give yourself totally to it because you're worrying about controlling the animal out there – and with a play like this you're never going to have total control. Here in the studio you can do fully whatever you think you would do.'

'When I read the play I couldn't believe it,' remembers Anna Calder-Marshall (Lavinia). 'I thought, "It gets worse and worse and worse." What's fascinating is that we've done it twice and the first time I found it utterly unbearable. I hate the word "Video Nasty" but someone said to me, "It's just like a video nasty, isn't it?" and it is very, very frightening. But this time, somehow, we've found – or I think we have – that the characters through the suffering get closer. Titus has committed the most appalling deeds and it isn't until he's maimed and his daughter's maimed that he learns anything about love.

'I know it's been done in a more stylised way, a colder way if you like [Jane Howell herself says that if she had been directing the play for the stage she might well have stylised the production more] but we felt you have to embrace the play and really go into it – which does mean quite a lot of upset.'

Of all the actors, Miss Calder-Marshall probably has the physically most gruesome and horrifying scenes to perform – raped and her hands cut off, her tongue cut out, she goes through a great deal of the play stained and bubbling blood, unable to communicate except by using her stumps and bloody mouth in the most painfully grotesque way. Scenes which on the page had seemed innocuous suddenly in the studio, at the sight of the delicate and gentle Miss Calder-Marshall reduced to such straits, took on a horror and pathos all the more wrenching for being unexpected. 'I'd seen an interview with Jonathan Miller,' she says, 'about a man who had Parkinson's disease and he refused to take any drugs and his passion was playing billiards. He said to Jonathan Miller, "The only way I can control myself is to run at a door very hard" – the impact shocked his body and then he would be able to go back, hold the cue and then shoot. The bravery of the man! The effort he had to make! And I was trying to think – if a woman was raped in Roman times it was the greatest shame that can happen, yet Lavinia has to find a way to tell Titus she's been raped and by whom, because he doesn't know what to do with his anger and she fears he's going out of his mind and so she has to do it . . . yet . . . [even in retrospect she is visibly moved by the scene she has just played] all these terrible things . . . it really got horribly nasty.

'Jane kept saying, "Draw back, Annie, preserve it," but it has the most extraordinary effect on you – you can't talk and your hands are taken away and just as an actress things build up inside you, you're trapped. It makes you work in a completely different way. It was very disturbing. The first time we rehearsed it I used to drive in thinking, "I'm going to be raped, I'm going to have my tongue cut out and my hands cut off," and there was this awful feeling in the pit of my stomach, I was living under this black, black cloud. This time . . . well, if you have an awful shock in your life, something really dreadful happens to you, you just think at the time, "This is awful," but maybe later you look back on it and think, "Well, of course, that should have happened to me because it's made me a better person in such and such a way . . .", and with this, after a year, one got a kind of distance on the play instead of just doing it. The first time it was too much, I know, for me, I couldn't channel it, it was crying all over the place. I know I'm crying quite a bit on this one,' she chuckles, 'but in the first production they called me "Old Flood-gates" – I just couldn't stop. It was like opening a wound and not finding a message . . . It was very good, we were all very excited by it, but for myself, personally, this time I hope it's more controlled. It's a very hard thing to be in control of.'

The character of Lavinia scarcely exists on the page except as a female chattel at the opening and then as a victim, but in playing it Miss Calder-Marshall found the role grew: 'She's not much there at the start of the play – a woman is an object in Rome, Lavinia is potty about Bassianus but then her father says, "You've got to marry the emperor because his word is law," and unlike Desdemona she doesn't say no, she goes along with it. I felt in a way Lavinia when she's got her tongue expresses herself less than when she hasn't got her tongue. The rape scene was hard but I accepted it because I thought she really does go from A to Z. But sometimes I thought, "I can't do it, it's getting worse and worse." Every night I've gone home to David [her husband, the actor David Burke] and said, "*That* was the vilest scene!"' At one point Lavinia has to exit with her father's lopped-off hand between her teeth. 'I went up to Cécile the other day and said, "What are you cooking?" and she said, "Chicken bones to put inside the hand so you've got something to get a hold of." It tastes awful! And the wretched blood . . . I haven't been able to eat.'

23

By contrast Hugh Quarshie, as Aaron the villainous Moor, has rather a good time in the play until he finally meets his come-uppance. He has played the part before, on stage at the RSC in John Barton's production, but then the play was heavily cut. Jane Howell's approach, he says, is 'vastly different'. In some interpretations Aaron becomes something of a demonic stage manager – he takes over the villainy from Tamora as the play progresses, masterminding all her and her sons' excesses. But he emerges, in Quarshie's performance, as a charismatic, almost sympathetic, figure. It is, on Quarshie's part, quite intentional – he sees Aaron as a figure of spontaneity and natural impulse, in direct opposition to the repressive, disciplined Romans. Both are cruel but the Romans' cruelty is 'civilised', made to conform to rigid social expectations. The impulse for me comes from the desire to dissociate myself entirely from any kind of Roman ethics, Western ethics, and to as it were purge myself from all that kind of consciousness, all that "conscience". That is precisely the thing that enslaves all the other characters. As he says to Lucius, "Thou . . . hast a thing within thee called a conscience": Aaron is a figure whose conscience isn't in any way trammelled by superstition, by some notion of divine retribution, very much of a freethinker. I'm playing him sticking to what I know, and what I know is that those of us who are called half-castes are rather more alive to the fact that moral values and aesthetic values are entirely relative, and that there are very few absolutes, and we resent that imposition of moral values upon us by those who consider them to be absolute. Put in other terms: Aaron isn't going to take any bullshit from any tight-arsed Roman. His last speech of defiance becomes not simply a denunciation of Roman values and not simply a celebration of Aaron's freedom from small-minded conscience, but also a determination to force Lucius to admit the truth – first of all that his Roman values are simply relative and secondly that they are simply a mask to cover the ugliness and violence of the Roman soul. Aaron's speech is an attempt to tear that mask away.' And indeed in Howell's production it is quite clear that the finally triumphant Lucius, Titus' surviving son, is, as Quarshie describes him, 'a repressed sadist', as ruthless as his father was, but with much more political savvy. Aaron's child, which the text has him promising to preserve, is displayed at the end in a coffin, the promise predictably broken.

Coming back to the play was, says Trevor Peacock, playing Titus, 'a great help, simply because I'm a great believer that you digest something – I had put it out of my mind, I'd written another show, I'd been playing for the RSC – but once you feed the computer it starts acting along certain lines. I became terribly aware of power men in the world, people like Yasser Arafat and Ronald Reagan, people who have this extraordinary power. An image came to me that he'd gone through a great deal, tired after ten years of killing people and looting and raping, and – I suppose it is a prefigurement of Lear – he has to learn all those lessons in a hard way. I do believe that sort of violence is in all of us. I imagine when *Titus* is shown people will say, "Oh, killing people and baking them!" But go to London airport now and buy a ticket to go in any one of sixty directions, wherever you arrive there will be something much, much, much worse than that going on at this minute in the world today, 1985: torture and persecution and violence of the most extreme kind is still there. We've learned so little.'

There are many problems in playing Titus, not least the exact degree to which he actually loses his mind. Peacock's performance traces a fascinatingly subtle line. 'It worried me for a long while,' he says, 'whether he was, how much he was faking – the whole business of whether one's mad. Again you think of Hamlet and Lear and the pretence and where the line comes and that strange area of not knowing whether you're mad or not, and one remembers that in Elizabethan England Tom of Bedlam and other psychopaths were all over the place, they weren't shut up, they were just everywhere. There must have been a great deal of it about. In the scene where Tamora pretends she is the spirit of Revenge, he says at the beginning to her, "I am not mad, I know thee well enough," and later he says to the audience, "I knew them all, though they suppos'd me mad," so clearly he is quite in charge of what's going on in his head. He must know that people think him mad. I decided in the end that he wasn't mad at all – he's in a very bad state but he's held on. The real turning-point, Jane carefully pointed out, was that when his sons' heads are brought in he says, "I have not another tear to shed . . . and besides if I cry I won't see my way to revenge" – he knows what he's got to do – I'll revenge you and you and you – and his road is clear. Yet he cannot seem to bring it about. The great tactician and military genius can't win this battle. And so he learns from Tamora. I always learn from my enemies, any good general does. The Goths operate in a subtle way – he remembers that in the first scene he enters as top dog and at the end of that twenty-minute scene Tamora is in charge of all Rome, power switches that quickly, and he thinks "I must do that", but he doesn't know how to operate in those ways; he's used to sticking cold steel into people and bullying them and sticking to his old-fashioned principles and he has to become like her in a way.'

The character, he points out, is a long way from us: 'In the hunt scene he's a bit worried but he's still a man in charge – he has that extraordinary line, "I have been troubled in my sleep" – and you think he just killed his son! One forgets he's a man who's wallowed in blood for a long while. We made a great point at the beginning of his coming in and saying twenty-one sons of his have died, and instead of saying, as we would, what a terrible disgrace that should be to me, he feels it's a great honour. And unfortunately for him in the middle of all these sons he had to sire a woman – well, that's too bad, and she's all right, and she's important because she will bear sons. We did an improvisation as though we were playing *The Godfather* because that's what they are like in a way. But it's through her that he begins to think, and it's a big part of the learning process. He's such a huge block of ice and he starts to melt. But it's too late for him. And his son Lucius seems to be even worse! The only hope is that grandson, whom Jane has very wisely placed as the dreamer who dreams this dream.'

'We're not into discussing much, Trevor and me,' says Howell. 'We just sort of do it and mutter at each other. The performance this year is much less mad than it was last year, and a lot of the scenes have shifted – especially the scene where he and his followers shoot arrows to the gods, which is probably the most difficult scene in the whole play to ding out exactly what is going on. I think this year it has much more logic. Last year it was about his being mad and I couldn't stand it. When we looked at it again we both thought it was wrong. What I think it is is a man who's very rigid, a general, very rigid of mind, a self-made general, so he always has a belief that the aristocracy is a shade better than he is. A man used to dealing with violence every day of his life, perpetrating it, seeing it perpetrated, believing rigidly in the code of law and Rome, the concept of Rome, the power of Rome, that it is right to be a colonising power. Then when events turn against his own family he has to learn lessons which are very hard, and he has no easy power of expression. I think in many scenes this is a man looking for expression. In the scene where Lavinia has her hands cut off he keeps saying, "What shall we do, what shall we do?" and I find that very moving. It's the process of a man who has to learn – he doesn't turn into a saint or anything like that, he doesn't transcend himself, but he does understand . . . that one shouldn't kill flies!' She laughs. 'I think in some ways it's a forerunner of *King Lear*, it's the same kind of madness – it's not a psychiatric madness, it's people pushed to the extreme searching for expressions of their feelings.

'A key line, I think, is when the boy Lucius says, "I have heard my grandsire say full oft Extremity of griefs would make men mad." Another key line is Trevor's: "When will this fearful slumber have an end?" That gave me the confidence to go ahead with this idea of a dream – the image is in the play. I didn't want to say: "Look, this is a dream" – it's not a play written as a dream. It's just my way into it is to think of it that way, so certain elements you've seen this morning, the smoke, the skull, certain of those elements will come in. It's a very good story and I've become more and more convinced that the play is by Shakespeare utterly, totally. I think the play is very subtle.'

THE BBC TV CAST AND PRODUCTION TEAM

The cast for the BBC Television production was as follows:

SATURNINUS	Brian Protheroe
BASSIANUS	Nicholas Gecks
TITUS ANDRONICUS	Trevor Peacock
MARCUS ANDRONICUS	Edward Hardwicke
LUCIUS	Gavin Richards
QUINTUS	Crispin Redman
MARTIUS	Tom Hunsinger
MUTIUS	Michael Packer
YOUNG LUCIUS	Paul Davies-Prowles
PUBLIUS	Paul Kelly
SEMPRONIUS	Derek Fuke
CAIUS	John Benfield
VALENTINE	Peter Searles
AEMILIUS	Walter Brown
ALARBUS	Peter Searles
DEMETRIUS	Neil McCaul
CHIRON	Michael Crompton
AARON	Hugh Quarshie
TAMORA	Eileen Atkins
LAVINIA	Anna Calder-Marshall
NURSE	Deddie Davies
CAPTAIN	Derek Fuke
MESSENGER	John Benfield
CLOWN	Tim Potter
1 GOTH	John Benfield
2 GOTH	Paul Kelly
3 GOTH	Derek Fuke
4 GOTH	Peter Searles

PRODUCTION MANAGER	Anthony Garrick
DIRECTOR'S ASSISTANT	Glenys Williams
PRODUCTION ASSOCIATE	Fraser Lowden

FIGHT ARRANGER	Malcolm Ranson
MUSIC	Dudley Simpson
LITERARY CONSULTANT	John Wilders
MAKE-UP ARTIST	Cécile Hay-Arthur
COSTUME DESIGNER	Colin Lavers
SOUND	Chick Anthony
LIGHTING	Sam Barclay
DESIGNER	Tony Burrough
PRODUCER	Shaun Sutton
DIRECTOR	Jane Howell

The production was recorded between 11 and 17 February 1985.

THE TEXT

Jane Howell

While there seems to be general agreement that *Titus Andronicus* is the first of Shakespeare's tragedies, there is considerable confusion over the author and the date of the first performance. Some scholars fix the first performance as 23 January 1594, while others argue that the play was being performed earlier. George Peele, a popular and established dramatist when Shakespeare began writing, is often credited as the author. The arguments in favour of this rest mainly on the inclusion of the word 'palliament' in the text. A palliament is a ceremonial garment worn to denote a candidate for election as emperor. Shakespeare does not use this word in any of the other Roman plays, while Peele had both coined the word and previously used it. There are also stylistic similarities in the play with other works by Peele. To sum up, the origins of the text are obscure, there is no definite date for the first performance and there is argument about authorship. The alternatives are: the play is by Peele; the play is by Peele, revised by Shakespeare; the play is a collaboration between the two; the play is by Shakespeare.

The sources for the story are, thankfully, much clearer. The Folger Institute Library has a volume entitled *The History of Titus Andronicus Renowned Roman General*. This book could easily have provided the basis of the plot. The additions to the original source material to be found in the play are interesting. Tamora is given a motive for her violent actions, when Titus kills her eldest son. Also Titus by this action creates the causes for his own suffering. Aaron in the original story is not developed; his love for his child, his scorn for religion, his energy, vitality and humour are all added by the author. Lucius, the eldest son of Titus, who eventually succeeds him, is also an addition. Another source for the text is the poet Ovid. Images from the story of Philomela are constantly referred to in the play. Philomela was raped by Tereus and the revenge of Progne was to serve Tereus a meal: he like Tamora ate his own sons.

Some of Shakespeare's plays, in particular *Titus* and *1 Henry VI*, are regarded with disdain by literary critics. However, both these plays are rooted in the physical craft of the theatre: Shakespeare, for let us presume, as I believe, that he did write these plays, is not writing at the height of his literary powers, but he does show an amazing knowledge of what works in a theatre. It is easier for people who know the craft of the playhouse to interpret them than literary academics. Within *Titus* the verse does soar from time to time, notably in Act III, and the depth of passion and philosophy in Act III Scene 2, with Titus' cry 'How if that fly had a father and mother?', leave me in little doubt as to the authorship of the play.

There are, however, some strange inconsistencies. A character who has just finished a scene may be required to begin the next one. This problem is very evident in the junction between Act III Scenes 1 and 2, and again between Act III Scene 2 and Act IV Scene 1. The opening of the play is also puzzling. Marcus has a speech, lines 18–45, in which he describes the death of Tamora's son, Alarbus, as an event which has already taken place, but later in the same scene we see Titus sacrificing the boy. In our production we took the liberty of rearranging the opening scene and placing Marcus' speech after the event described. This allowed us to begin the play with Titus and to develop the ceremonial of Rome, thus giving the audience a chance to relate to the main protagonist from the beginning of the play, and giving them a glimpse of the nature of Roman society, in which violence is ritualised and death is to 'sleep in fame'. The original opening of the play was a violent argument between Saturninus and Bassianus, an abrupt beginning which gives the audience scant chance to identify these characters, and more importantly to realise that their father, the Emperor, is dead and there is a power vacuum in Rome. The only other liberty that we have taken was to increase the number of appearances of Young Lucius, so that he assumes the role of a silent watcher of events.

The text of the play, printed here in full, is that prepared by Professor Peter Alexander for his celebrated 1951 edition of the *Complete Works*. This edition was used for all the plays in the BBC series. In the textual notes in the right-hand margin, I have indicated a private conversation between two actors, which is not overheard by the other players, by the word 'Aside'. Lines spoken directly to the audience are indicated by the words 'Spoken to camera'. Cuts, which were usually made for reasons of repetition or obscurity, are also marked. The scene numbers follow the changes of location used in the television production. The notes describing specific actions are to direct the attention of the reader to the meaning and atmosphere we attempt to express with each scene.

TITUS ANDRONICUS

DRAMATIS PERSONÆ

SATURNINUS, *son to the late Emperor of Rome, afterwards Emperor.*
BASSIANUS, *brother to Saturninus.*
TITUS ANDRONICUS, *a noble Roman.*
MARCUS ANDRONICUS, *Tribune of the People, and brother to* TITUS.
LUCIUS,
QUINTUS, } *sons to Titus*
MARTIUS, } *Andronicus.*
MUTIUS,
YOUNG LUCIUS, *a boy, son to Lucius.*
PUBLIUS, *son to Marcus Andronicus.*
SEMPRONIUS,
CAIUS, } *kinsmen to Titus.*
VALENTINE,

ÆMILIUS, *a noble Roman.*
ALARBUS
DEMETRIUS, } *sons to Tamora.*
CHIRON,
AARON, *a Moor, beloved by Tamora.*
A CAPTAIN.
A MESSENGER.
A CLOWN.

TAMORA, *Queen of the Goths.*
LAVINIA, *daughter to Titus Andronicus.*
A NURSE, *and a black* CHILD.

ROMANS *and* GOTHS, SENATORS, TRIBUNES, OFFICERS, SOLDIERS, *and* ATTENDANTS.

All non-speaking parts wear masks as they have no dramatic function in the play, unlike the citizens in *Julius Caesar*. This is a reflection of the society portrayed, an autocracy in which the people were powerless.

The television production begins at line 64 (page 35) and continues to line 168 (page 37), then returning to line 1.

THE SCENE : *Rome and the neighbourhood.*

ACT ONE

SCENE I. *Rome. Before the Capitol.*

Flourish. Enter the TRIBUNES *and* SENATORS *aloft ; and then enter below* SATURNINUS *and his* FOLLOWERS *at one door, and* BASSIANUS *and his* FOLLOWERS *at the other, with drums and trumpets.*

SAT. Noble patricians, patrons of my right,
Defend the justice of my cause with arms ;
And, countrymen, my loving followers,
Plead my successive title with your swords.
I am his first-born son that was the last   5
That ware the imperial diadem of Rome ;
Then let my father's honours live in me,
Nor wrong mine age with this indignity.
BAS. Romans, friends, followers, favourers of my right,
If ever Bassianus, Cæsar's son,   10
Were gracious in the eyes of royal Rome,
Keep then this passage to the Capitol ;
And suffer not dishonour to approach
The imperial seat, to virtue consecrate,
To justice, continence, and nobility ;   15
But let desert in pure election shine ;
And, Romans, fight for freedom in your choice.

SCENE 3
A Public Place in Rome.
SATURNINUS and BASSIANUS march towards each other followed by their supporters. BASSIANUS guards the passage to the Capitol.

BASSIANUS and SATURNINUS draw their swords.

Bassianus (Nicholas Gecks) and Saturninus (Brian Protheroe) confront each other

Trevor Peacock as Titus

Enter MARCUS ANDRONICUS *aloft, with the crown.*

MARC. Princes, that strive by factions and by friends
    Ambitiously for rule and empery,
    Know that the people of Rome, for whom we stand   20
    A special party, have by common voice
    In election for the Roman empery
    Chosen Andronicus, surnamed Pius
    For many good and great deserts to Rome.
    A nobler man, a braver warrior,   25
    Lives not this day within the city walls.
    He by the Senate is accited home,
    From weary wars against the barbarous Goths,
    That with his sons, a terror to our foes,
    Hath yok'd a nation strong, train'd up in arms.   30
    Ten years are spent since first he undertook
    This cause of Rome, and chastised with arms
    Our enemies' pride ; five times he hath return'd
    Bleeding to Rome, bearing his valiant sons
    In coffins from the field ; *and at this day*   35
    To the monument of that Andronici
    Done sacrifice of expiation,
    And slain the noblest prisoner of the Goths.
    And now at last, laden with honour's spoils,
    Returns the good Andronicus to Rome,
    Renowned Titus, flourishing in arms.
    Let us entreat, by honour of his name
    Whom worthily you would have now succeed,   40
    And in the Capitol and Senate's right,
    Whom you pretend to honour and adore,
    That you withdraw you and abate your strength,
    Dismiss your followers, and, as suitors should,
    Plead your deserts in peace and humbleness.   45
SAT. How fair the Tribune speaks to calm my thoughts.
BAS. Marcus Andronicus, so I do affy
    In thy uprightness and integrity,
    And so I love and honour thee and thine,
    Thy noble brother Titus and his sons,   50
    And her to whom my thoughts are humbled all,
    Gracious Lavinia, Rome's rich ornament,
    That I will here dismiss my loving friends,
    And to my fortunes and the people's favour
    Commit my cause in balance to be weigh'd.   55
              [Exeunt the soldiers of Bassianus.
SAT. Friends, that have been thus forward in my right,
    I thank you all and here dismiss you all,
    And to the love and favour of my country
    Commit myself, my person, and the cause.
              [Exeunt the soldiers of Saturninus.
    Rome, be as just and gracious unto me   60
    As I am confident and kind to thee.
    Open the gates and let me in.
BAS. Tribunes, and me, a poor competitor.
           [Flourish. They go up into the Senate House.

Soldiers prevent BASSIANUS and SATURNINUS from fighting. MARCUS holds the sceptre taken from the dead Emperor, indicating that power now resides with him, AEMILIUS and the tribunes who accompany him.

MARCUS passes the prisoners, TAMORA, her sons and AARON.

Line 46 spoken to camera.

SATURNINUS and BASSIANUS take white robes from PUBLIUS, signifying that they are candidates for election as Emperor.

A drum is heard. They turn to see TITUS returning from the Mausoleum. No stage direction. The production continues without a break at line 169 (page 37).

Enter a CAPTAIN.

CAP. Romans, make way. The good Andronicus,
  Patron of virtue, Rome's best champion,   65
  Successful in the battles that he fights,
  With honour and with fortune is return'd
  From where he circumscribed with his sword
  And brought to yoke the enemies of Rome.

Sound drums and trumpets, and then enter MARTIUS *and* MUTIUS, *two of
Titus' sons ; and then two* MEN *bearing a coffin covered with black ;
then* LUCIUS *and* QUINTUS, *two other sons ; then* TITUS ANDRONICUS ;
and then TAMORA *the Queen of Goths, with her three sons,* ALARBUS,
DEMETRIUS *and* CHIRON, *with* AARON *the Moor, and* OTHERS, *as
many as can be. Then set down the coffin and* TITUS *speaks.*

TIT. Hail, Rome, victorious in thy mourning weeds !   70
  Lo, as the bark that hath discharg'd her fraught
  Returns with precious lading to the bay
  From whence at first she weigh'd her anchorage,
  Cometh Andronicus, bound with laurel boughs,
| To re-salute his country with his tears,   75 |
| Tears of true joy for his return to Rome.
  Thou great defender of this Capitol,
  Stand gracious to the rites that we intend !
  Romans, of five and twenty valiant sons,
  Half of the number that King Priam had,   80
  Behold the poor remains, alive and dead !
  These that survive let Rome reward with love ;
  These that I bring unto their latest home,
  With burial amongst their ancestors.
  Here Goths have given me leave to sheathe my sword. 85
  Titus, unkind, and careless of thine own,
  Why suffer'st thou thy sons, unburied yet,
  To hover on the dreadful shore of Styx ?
  Make way to lay them by their brethren.   [*They open the tomb.*
  There greet in silence, as the dead are wont,   90
  And sleep in peace, slain in your country's wars.
  O sacred receptacle of my joys,
  Sweet cell of virtue and nobility,
  How many sons hast thou of mine in store
  That thou wilt never render to me more !   95
LUC. Give us the proudest prisoner of the Goths,
  That we may hew his limbs, and on a pile
  Ad manes fratrum sacrifice his flesh
  Before this earthy prison of their bones,
  That so the shadows be not unappeas'd,   100
  Nor we disturb'd with prodigies on earth.
TIT. I give him you—the noblest that survives,
  The eldest son of this distressed queen.
TAM. Stay, Roman brethren ! Gracious conqueror,
  Victorious Titus, rue the tears I shed,   105
  A mother's tears in passion for her son ;
  And if thy sons were ever dear to thee,
  O, think my son to be as dear to me !

SCENE I
*A Public Place in
Rome.*
YOUNG LUCIUS watches
as the dead Emperor is
carried in procession,
accompanied by
BASSIANUS and
SATURNINUS. MARCUS
takes the sceptre, the
symbol of power, from
the Emperor. As the
procession moves off
the CAPTAIN speaks.

Four dead sons of
TITUS are carried in,
followed by the
prisoners. YOUNG
LUCIUS brings a bowl of
water to TITUS so that
he may wash his hands
before approaching the
altar.

After line 75: TITUS
lights a ceremonial
flame on the altar.

As TITUS sheathes his
sword he staggers.

Two of TITUS' sons, led
by LUCIUS, march
forward to supervise
the opening of huge
iron gates at the
entrance to the
Mausoleum of the
Andronicus family.

As one of TITUS' sons
drags ALARBUS forward
to the altar, TAMORA
interrupts the
ceremony.

Sufficeth not that we are brought to Rome
To beautify thy triumphs, and return   110
Captive to thee and to thy Roman yoke ;
But must my sons be slaughtered in the streets
For valiant doings in their country's cause ?
O, if to fight for king and commonweal
Were piety in thine, it is in these.   115
Andronicus, stain not thy tomb with blood.
Wilt thou draw near the nature of the gods ?
Draw near them then in being merciful.
Sweet mercy is nobility's true badge.
Thrice-noble Titus, spare my first-born son.   120   TAMORA kneels to
TIT. Patient yourself, madam, and pardon me.   TITUS.
These are their brethren, whom your Goths beheld
Alive and dead ; and for their brethren slain
Religiously they ask a sacrifice.
To this your son is mark'd, and die he must   125   TITUS' sons tear
T' appease their groaning shadows that are gone.   ALARBUS' shirt. TITUS
LUC. Away with him, and make a fire straight ;   nicks him with a
And with our swords, upon a pile of wood,   dagger and draws
Let's hew his limbs till they be clean consum'd.   blood.
                  [Exeunt TITUS' SONS, with ALARBUS.
TAM. O cruel, irreligious piety !   130
CHI. Was never Scythia half so barbarous !
DEM. Oppose not Scythia to ambitious Rome.
Alarbus goes to rest, and we survive
To tremble under Titus' threat'ning look.
Then, madam, stand resolv'd, but hope withal   135
The self-same gods that arm'd the Queen of Troy
With opportunity of sharp revenge
Upon the Thracian tyrant in his tent
May favour Tamora, the Queen of Goths—
When Goths were Goths and Tamora was queen—   140
To quit the bloody wrongs upon her foes.

       Re-enter LUCIUS, QUINTUS, MARTIUS, and MUTIUS,   TITUS' sons return,
        the sons of Andronicus, with their swords bloody.   their faces daubed with
                                              ritual markings and
LUC. See, lord and father, how we have perform'd   holding out hands
Our Roman rites : Alarbus' limbs are lopp'd,   covered in blood.
And entrails feed the sacrificing fire,   LUCIUS throws entrails
Whose smoke like incense doth perfume the sky.   145   on to the altar fire.
Remaineth nought but to inter our brethren,
And with loud 'larums welcome them to Rome.
TIT. Let it be so, and let Andronicus   TITUS leads a
Make this his latest farewell to their souls.   procession off into the
                                            Mausoleum.
         [Sound trumpets and lay the coffin in the tomb.

                                          SCENE 2
In peace and honour rest you here, my sons ;   150   *The Mausoleum of the*
Rome's readiest champions, repose you here in rest,   *Andronici.*
Secure from worldly chances and mishaps !   TITUS and his family
Here lurks no treason, here no envy swells,   circle the Mausoleum
Here grow no damned drugs, here are no storms,   passing the bodies of
No noise, but silence and eternal sleep.   155   generations of dead.
                                            His four dead sons lie
                                          before an altar. YOUNG
                                          LUCIUS lights four
                                          candles. Then TITUS
                             36   speaks.

In peace and honour rest you here, my sons !

Enter LAVINIA.

LAV. In peace and honour live Lord Titus long ;

LAVINIA gives TITUS a phial of her tears. He sprinkles them on the altar.

My noble lord and father, live in fame !
Lo, at this tomb my tributary tears
I render for my brethren's obsequies ;   160
And at thy feet I kneel, with tears of joy
Shed on this earth for thy return to Rome.
O, bless me here with thy victorious hand,
Whose fortunes Rome's best citizens applaud !
TIT. Kind Rome, that hast thus lovingly reserv'd   165
The cordial of mine age to glad my heart !
Lavinia, live ; outlive thy father's days,
And fame's eternal date, for virtue's praise !

A sudden noise is heard.

Enter, above, MARCUS ANDRONICUS *and* TRIBUNES ; *re-enter*
SATURNINUS, BASSIANUS, *and* ATTENDANTS.

No stage direction. Scene 3 (page 32) follows. Line 169 continues after line 63 without a break.

MARC. Long live Lord Titus, my beloved brother,
Gracious triumpher in the eyes of Rome !   170
TIT. Thanks, gentle Tribune, noble brother Marcus.
MARC. And welcome, nephews, from successful wars,
You that survive and you that sleep in fame.
Fair lords, your fortunes are alike in all
That in your country's service drew your swords ;   175
But safer triumph is this funeral pomp

Lines 174–178 omitted.

That hath aspir'd to Solon's happiness
And triumphs over chance in honour's bed.
Titus Andronicus, the people of Rome,
Whose friend in justice thou hast ever been,   180
Send thee by me, their Tribune and their trust,
This palliament of white and spotless hue ;
And name thee in election for the empire
With these our late-deceased Emperor's sons :

PUBLIUS brings a white robe and offers it to TITUS.

Be candidatus then, and put it on,   185
And help to set a head on headless Rome.
TIT. A better head her glorious body fits
Than his that shakes for age and feebleness.
What should I don this robe and trouble you ?
Be chosen with proclamations to-day,   190
To-morrow yield up rule, resign my life,
And set abroad new business for you all ?
Rome, I have been thy soldier forty years,
And led my country's strength successfully,
And buried one and twenty valiant sons,   195
Knighted in field, slain manfully in arms,
In right and service of their noble country.
Give me a staff of honour for mine age,
But not a sceptre to control the world.
Upright he held it, lords, that held it last.   200
MARC. Titus, thou shalt obtain and ask the empery.
SAT. Proud and ambitious Tribune, canst thou tell ?
TIT. Patience, Prince Saturninus.

SAT.   Romans, do me right.
  Patricians, draw your swords, and sheathe them not
  Till Saturninus be Rome's Emperor.   205
  Andronicus, would thou were shipp'd to hell
  Rather than rob me of the people's hearts !
LUC. Proud Saturnine, interrupter of the good
  That noble-minded Titus means to thee !
TIT. Content thee, Prince ; I will restore to thee   210
  The people's hearts, and wean them from themselves.
BAS. Andronicus, I do not flatter thee,
  But honour thee, and will do till I die.
  My faction if thou strengthen with thy friends,
  I will most thankful be , and thanks to men   215
  Of noble minds is honourable meed.
TIT. People of Rome, and people's Tribunes here,
  I ask your voices and your suffrages :
  Will ye bestow them friendly on Andronicus ?
TRIB. To gratify the good Andronicus,   220
  And gratulate his safe return to Rome,
  The people will accept whom he admits.
TIT. Tribunes, I thank you ; and this suit I make,
  That you create our Emperor's eldest son,
  Lord Saturnine ; whose virtues will, I hope,   225
  Reflect on Rome as Titan's rays on earth,
  And ripen justice in this commonweal.
  Then, if you will elect by my advice,
  Crown him, and say ' Long live our Emperor ! '
MARC. With voices and applause of every sort,   230
  Patricians and plebeians, we create
  Lord Saturninus Rome's great Emperor ;
  And say ' Long live our Emperor Saturnine ! '
            [*A long flourish till they come down.*
SAT. Titus Andronicus, for thy favours done
  To us in our election this day   235
  I give thee thanks in part of thy deserts,
  And will with deeds requite thy gentleness ;
  And for an onset, Titus, to advance
  Thy name and honourable family,
  Lavinia will I make my emperess,   240
  Rome's royal mistress, mistress of my heart,
  And in the sacred Pantheon her espouse.
  Tell me, Andronicus, doth this motion please thee ?
TIT. It doth, my worthy lord, and in this match
  I hold me highly honoured of your Grace,   245
  And here in sight of Rome, to Saturnine,
  King and commander of our commonweal,
  The wide world's Emperor, do I consecrate
  My sword, my chariot, and my prisoners,
  Presents well worthy Rome's imperious lord;   250
  Receive them then, the tribute that I owe,
  Mine honour's ensigns humbled at thy feet.
SAT. Thanks, noble Titus, father of my life.
  How proud I am of thee and of thy gifts
  Rome shall record ; and when I do forget   255

Stage directions (right column):

SATURNINUS draws his sword.

Flanked by MARCUS and AEMILIUS, TITUS addresses the people of Rome from the steps leading to the throne.

TITUS takes a laurel-wreath crown from the throne and gives it to SATURNINUS, who ascends to the throne. They kneel as he places the wreath on his head.

LAVINIA ascends to the throne and kisses SATURNINUS' hand.

TITUS, TAMORA, her sons and AARON kneel at SATURNINUS' feet.

The least of these unspeakable deserts,
Romans, forget your fealty to me.
TIT. [*To Tamora*] Now, madam, are you prisoner to an emperor;
  To him that for your honour and your state
  Will use you nobly and your followers.   260
SAT. [*Aside.*] A goodly lady, trust me; of the hue | Not spoken aside.
  That I would choose, were I to choose anew.—
  Clear up, fair Queen, that cloudy countenance;
  Though chance of war hath wrought this change of cheer,
  Thou com'st not to be made a scorn in Rome—   265
  Princely shall be thy usage every way.
  Rest on my word, and let not discontent
  Daunt all your hopes. Madam, he comforts you
  Can make you greater than the Queen of Goths.
  Lavinia, you are not displeas'd with this?   270
LAV. Not I, my lord, sith true nobility
  Warrants these words in princely courtesy.
SAT. Thanks, sweet Lavinia. Romans, let us go.
  Ransomless here we set our prisoners free.   TAMORA kisses
  Proclaim our honours, lords, with trump and drum. [*Flourish.* SATURNINUS' hand. As
BAS. Lord Titus, by your leave, this maid is mine. [*Seizing Lavinia.* TITUS and LAVINIA
TIT. How, sir! Are you in earnest then, my lord?   leave, SATURNINUS
BAS. Ay, noble Titus, and resolv'd withal   supervises the release
  To do myself this reason and this right.   of the prisoners.
MARC. Suum cuique is our Roman justice: 280
  This prince in justice seizeth but his own.
LUC. And that he will and shall, if Lucius live.
TIT. Traitors, avaunt! Where is the Emperor's guard?
  Treason, my lord—Lavinia is surpris'd!
SAT. Surpris'd! By whom?
BAS.   By him that justly may   285
  Bear his betroth'd from all the world away.
        [*Exeunt* BASSIANUS *and* MARCUS *with* LAVINIA.

MUT. Brothers, help to convey her hence away,
  And with my sword I'll keep this door safe.
        [*Exeunt* LUCIUS, QUINTUS, *and* MARTIUS.

TIT. Follow, my lord, and I'll soon bring her back.
MUT. My lord, you pass not here.
TIT.   What, villain boy!   290
  Bar'st me my way in Rome?
MUT.   Help, Lucius, help!
    [TITUS *kills him. During the fray, exeunt* SATURNINUS, TITUS kills MUTIUS with
        TAMORA, DEMETRIUS, CHIRON *and* AARON. his dagger. MARCUS,
                                      LUCIUS and the sons
          Re-enter LUCIUS.   return when they hear
                                        MUTIUS' cries for help.
LUC. My lord, you are unjust, and more than so:
  In wrongful quarrel you have slain your son.
TIT. Nor thou nor he are any sons of mine;
  My sons would never so dishonour me.   295

       Re-enter aloft the EMPEROR *with* TAMORA | SATURNINUS is still
       and her two SONS, *and* AARON *the Moor.* | with TAMORA on the
                                         steps of the throne.

Traitor, restore Lavinia to the Emperor.
LUC. Dead, if you will ; but not to be his wife,
    That is another's lawful promis'd love.   [*Exit.*
SAT. No, Titus, no ; the Emperor needs her not,
    Nor her, nor thee, nor any of thy stock.   300
    I'll trust by leisure him that mocks me once ;
    Thee never, nor thy traitorous haughty sons,
    Confederates all thus to dishonour me.
    Was there none else in Rome to make a stale
    But Saturnine ? Full well, Andronicus,   305
    Agree these deeds with that proud brag of thine
    That saidst I begg'd the empire at thy hands.
TIT. O monstrous ! What reproachful words are these ?
SAT. But go thy ways ; go, give that changing piece
    To him that flourish'd for her with his sword.   310
    A valiant son-in-law thou shalt enjoy ;
    One fit to bandy with thy lawless sons,
    To ruffle in the commonwealth of Rome.
TIT. These words are razors to my wounded heart.
SAT. And therefore, lovely Tamora, Queen of Goths,   315
    That, like the stately Phœbe 'mongst her nymphs,
    Dost overshine the gallant'st dames of Rome,
    If thou be pleas'd with this my sudden choice,
    Behold, I choose thee, Tamora, for my bride
    And will create thee Emperess of Rome.   320
    Speak, Queen of Goths, dost thou applaud my choice ?
    And here I swear by all the Roman gods—
    Sith priest and holy water are so near,
    And tapers burn so bright, and everything
    In readiness for Hymenæus stand—   325
    I will not re-salute the streets of Rome,
    Or climb my palace, till from forth this place
    I lead espous'd my bride along with me.
TAM. And here in sight of heaven to Rome I swear,
    If Saturnine advance the Queen of Goths,   330
    She will a handmaid be to his desires,
    A loving nurse, a mother to his youth.
SAT. Ascend, fair queen, Pantheon. Lords, accompany
    Your noble Emperor and his lovely bride,
    Sent by the heavens for Prince Saturnine,   335
    Whose wisdom hath her fortune conquered ;
    There shall we consummate our spousal rites.
                 [*Exeunt all but Titus.*
TIT. I am not bid to wait upon this bride.
    Titus, when wert thou wont to walk alone,
    Dishonoured thus, and challenged of wrongs ?   340

      Re-enter MARCUS, *and Titus' sons*, LUCIUS,
          QUINTUS, *and* MARTIUS.

MARC. O Titus, see, O, see what thou hast done !
    In a bad quarrel slain a virtuous son.
TIT. No, foolish Tribune, no ; no son of mine—
    Nor thou, nor these, confederates in the deed
    That hath dishonoured all our family ;   345

TITUS' sons draw their
swords and threaten
their father.

Only SATURNINUS,
TAMORA, her sons and
AARON exit.

Lines 338–340 spoken
to camera.

They have been
present throughout.

Unworthy brother and unworthy sons !
LUC. But let us give him burial, as becomes ;
　　Give Mutius burial with our bretheren.
TIT. Traitors, away !　He rests not in this tomb.
　　This monument five hundred years hath stood,　　　　350　　TITUS stands in front of
　　Which I have sumptuously re-edified ;　　　　　　　　　　　　the gates to the
　　Here none but soldiers and Rome's servitors　　　　　　　　Mausoleum.
　　Repose in fame ;　none basely slain in brawls.
　　Bury him where you can, he comes not here.
MARC. My lord, this is impiety in you.　　　　　　　　　　355
　　My nephew Mutius' deeds do plead for him ;
　　He must be buried with his bretheren.
QUIN. ⎫
MART. ⎭ And shall, or him we will accompany.　　　　　　　　MARTIUS does not
TIT. 'And shall' !　What villain was it spake that word ?　　　speak.
QUIN. He that would vouch it in any place but here.　　　360
TIT. What, would you bury him in my despite ?
MARC. No, noble Titus, but entreat of thee
　　To pardon Mutius and to bury him.
TIT. Marcus, even thou hast struck upon my crest,
　　And with these boys mine honour thou hast wounded.　365
　　My foes I do repute you every one ;
　　So trouble me no more, but get you gone.
MART. He is not with himself ; let us withdraw.
QUIN. Not I, till Mutius' bones be buried.
　　　　　　　　　　　　[The BROTHER and the SONS kneel.　370
MARC. Brother, for in that name doth nature plead—
QUIN. Father, and in that name doth nature speak—
TIT. Speak thou no more, if all the rest will speed.
MARC. Renowned Titus, more than half my soul—
LUC. Dear father, soul and substance of us all—
MARC. Suffer thy brother Marcus to inter　　　　　　　　　375
　　His noble nephew here in virtue's nest,
　　That died in honour and Lavinia's cause.
　　Thou art a Roman—be not barbarous.
　　The Greeks upon advice did bury Ajax,
　　That slew himself ; and wise Laertes' son　　　　　　　　380
　　Did graciously plead for his funerals.
　　Let not young Mutius, then, that was thy joy,
　　Be barr'd his entrance here.
TIT.　　　　　　　　　　Rise, Marcus, rise ;　　　　　　　　MARCUS kneels to
　　The dismal'st day is this that e'er I saw,　　　　　　　　TITUS.
　　To be dishonoured by my sons in Rome !　　　　　　385
　　Well, bury him, and bury me the next.
　　　　　　　　　　　　[They put Mutius in the tomb.　　As MUTIUS is carried to
LUC. There lie thy bones, sweet Mutius, with thy friends,　the tomb, YOUNG
　　Till we with trophies do adorn thy tomb.　　　　　　　LUCIUS picks up the
ALL. [Kneeling.]　No man shed tears for noble Mutius　　dagger used to kill him
　　He lives in fame that died in virtue's cause.　　　　　390　and stares at his
MARC. My lord—to step out of these dreary dumps—　　grandfather, who turns
　　How comes it that the subtle Queen of Goths　　　　　away.
　　Is of a sudden thus advanc'd in Rome ?
TIT. I know not, Marcus, but I know it is—
　　Whether by device or no, the heavens can tell.　　　　395

Is she not, then, beholding to the man
That brought her for this high good turn so far ?
MARC. Yes, and will nobly him remunerate.

Flourish. Re-enter the EMPEROR, TAMORA *and her two* SONS, *with the*
MOOR, *at one door ; at the other door,* BASSIANUS *and* LAVINIA,
with OTHERS.

BASSIANUS and LAVINIA
kneel to ask TITUS'
pardon as SATURNINUS
returns in formal
procession with his
new wife, TAMORA.

SAT. So, Bassianus, you have play'd your prize :
   God give you joy, sir, of your gallant bride !   400
BAS. And you of yours, my lord ! I say no more,
   Nor wish no less ; and so I take my leave.
SAT. Traitor, if Rome have law or we have power,
   Thou and thy faction shall repent this rape.
BAS. Rape, call you it, my lord, to seize my own,   405
   My true betrothed love, and now my wife ?
   But let the laws of Rome determine all ;
   Meanwhile am I possess'd of that is mine.
SAT. 'Tis good, sir. You are very short with us ;
   But if we live we'll be as sharp with you.   410
BAS. My lord, what I have done, as best I may,
   Answer I must, and shall do with my life.
   Only thus much I give your Grace to know :
   By all the duties that I owe to Rome,
   This noble gentleman, Lord Titus here,   415
   Is in opinion and in honour wrong'd,
   That, in the rescue of Lavinia,
   With his own hand did slay his youngest son,
   In zeal to you, and highly mov'd to wrath
   To be controll'd in that he frankly gave.   420
   Receive him then to favour, Saturnine,
   That hath express'd himself in all his deeds
   A father and a friend to thee and Rome.
TIT. Prince Bassianus, leave to plead my deeds.
   'Tis thou and those that have dishonoured me.   425
   Rome and the righteous heavens be my judge
   How I have lov'd and honoured Saturnine !
TAM. My worthy lord, if ever Tamora
   Were gracious in those princely eyes of thine,
   Then hear me speak indifferently for all ;   430
   And at my suit, sweet, pardon what is past.
SAT. What, madam ! be dishonoured openly,
   And basely put it up without revenge ?
TAM. Not so, my lord ; the gods of Rome forfend
   I should be author to dishonour you !   435
   But on mine honour dare I undertake
   For good Lord Titus' innocence in all,
   Whose fury not dissembled speaks his griefs.
   Then at my suit look graciously on him ;
   Lose not so noble a friend on vain suppose,   440
   Nor with sour looks afflict his gentle heart.
   [*Aside to* SAT.] My lord, be rul'd by me, be won at last ;
   Dissemble all your griefs and discontents.
   You are but newly planted in your throne ;
   Lest, then, the people, and patricians too,   445

Lines 442–449 spoken
aside to SATURNINUS.

Upon a just survey take Titus' part,
And so supplant you for ingratitude,
Which Rome reputes to be a heinous sin,
Yield at entreats, and then let me alone :
I'll find a day to massacre them all,   450
And raze their faction and their family,
The cruel father and his traitorous sons,
To whom I sued for my dear son's life ;
And make them know what 'tis to let a queen
Kneel in the streets and beg for grace in vain.—   455
Come, come, sweet Emperor ; come, Andronicus.
Take up this good old man, and cheer the heart
That dies in tempest of thy angry frown.
SAT. Rise, Titus, rise ; my Empress hath prevail'd.
TIT. I thank your Majesty and her, my lord ;   460
These words, these looks, infuse new life in me.
TAM. Titus, I am incorporate in Rome,
A Roman now adopted happily,
And must advise the Emperor for his good.
This day all quarrels die, Andronicus ;   465
And let it be mine honour, good my lord,
That I have reconcil'd your friends and you.
For you, Prince Bassianus, I have pass'd
My word and promise to the Emperor
That you will be more mild and tractable.   470
And fear not, lords—and you, Lavinia.
By my advice, all humbled on your knees,
You shall ask pardon of his Majesty.
LUC. We do, and vow to heaven and to his Highness
That what we did was mildly as we might,   475
Tend'ring our sister's honour and our own.
MARC. That on mine honour here do I protest.
SAT. Away, and talk not ; trouble us no more.
TAM. Nay, nay, sweet Emperor, we must all be friends.
The Tribune and his nephews kneel for grace.   480
I will not be denied.   Sweet heart, look back.
SAT. Marcus, for thy sake, and thy brother's here,
And at my lovely Tamora's entreats,
I do remit these young men's heinous faults.
Stand up.   485
Lavinia, though you left me like a churl,
I found a friend ; and sure as death I swore
I would not part a bachelor from the priest.
Come, if the Emperor's court can feast two brides,
You are my guest, Lavinia, and your friends.   490
This day shall be a love-day, Tamora.
TIT. To-morrow, an it please your Majesty
To hunt the panther and the hart with me,
With horn and hound we'll give your Grace bonjour.
SAT. Be it so, Titus, and gramercy too.   [*Exeunt. Sound trumpets.*

Lines 442–449 spoken aside.

Lines 450–455 spoken to camera.

LUCIUS, LAVINIA and BASSIANUS kneel.
MARCUS, QUINTUS and MARTIUS kneel.

As they leave LUCIUS embraces his son, YOUNG LUCIUS. AARON watches from the walls.

43

ACT TWO

SCENE I. *Rome. Before the palace.*

Enter AARON.

AAR. Now climbeth Tamora Olympus' top,
Safe out of Fortune's shot, and sits aloft,
Secure of thunder's crack or lightning flash,
Advanc'd above pale envy's threat'ning reach.
As when the golden sun salutes the morn,   5
And, having gilt the ocean with his beams,
Gallops the zodiac in his glistening coach
And overlooks the highest-peering hills,
So Tamora.
Upon her wit doth earthly honour wait,   10
And virtue stoops and trembles at her frown.
Then, Aaron, arm thy heart and fit thy thoughts
To mount aloft with thy imperial mistress,
And mount her pitch whom thou in triumph long
Hast prisoner held, fett'red in amorous chains,   15
And faster bound to Aaron's charming eyes
Than is Prometheus tied to Caucasus.
Away with slavish weeds and servile thoughts!
I will be bright and shine in pearl and gold,
To wait upon this new-made emperess.   20
To wait, said I ? To wanton with this queen,
This goddess, this Semiramis, this nymph,
This siren that will charm Rome's Saturnine,
And see his shipwreck and his commonweal's.
Hullo! what storm is this ?   25

Enter CHIRON *and* DEMETRIUS, *braving.*

DEM. Chiron, thy years wants wit, thy wits wants edge
And manners, to intrude where I am grac'd,
And may, for aught thou knowest, affected be.
CHI. Demetrius, thou dost over-ween in all ;
And so in this, to bear me down with braves.   30
'Tis not the difference of a year or two
Makes me less gracious or thee more fortunate :
I am as able and as fit as thou
To serve and to deserve my mistress' grace ;
And that my sword upon thee shall approve,   35
And plead my passions for Lavinia's love.
AAR. [*Aside.*] Clubs, clubs! These lovers will not keep the peace.
DEM. Why, boy, although our mother, unadvis'd,
Gave you a dancing-rapier by your side,
Are you so desperate grown to threat your friends ?   40
Go to ; have your lath glued within your sheath
Till you know better how to handle it.
CHI. Meanwhile, sir, with the little skill I have,
Full well shalt thou perceive how much I dare.
DEM. Ay, boy, grow ye so brave ?   [*They draw.*

SCENE 4
*Within the Emperor's
Palace.*

Lines 1–25 spoken to
camera.

DEMETRIUS drags
CHIRON and throws
him down on the steps.
For 'wits' read 'wit'.

Line 37 spoken to
camera.

AAR. [*Coming forward.*]   Why, how now, lords !   45
  So near the Emperor's palace dare ye draw
  And maintain such a quarrel openly ?
  Full well I wot the ground of all this grudge :
  I would not for a million of gold
  The cause were known to them it most concerns ;   50
  Nor would your noble mother for much more
  Be so dishonoured in the court of Rome.
  For shame, put up.
DEM.   Not I, till I have sheath'd
  My rapier in his bosom, and withal
  Thrust those reproachful speeches down his throat   55
  That he hath breath'd in my dishonour here.
CHI. For that I am prepar'd and full resolv'd,
  Foul-spoken coward, that thund'rest with thy tongue,
  And with thy weapon nothing dar'st perform.
AAR. Away, I say !   60
  Now, by the gods that warlike Goths adore,
  This pretty brabble will undo us all.
  Why, lords, and think you not how dangerous
  It is to jet upon a prince's right ?
  What, is Lavinia then become so loose,   65
  Or Bassianus so degenerate,
  That for her love such quarrels may be broach'd
  Without controlment, justice, or revenge ?
  Young lords, beware ; an should the Empress know
  This discord's ground, the music would not please.   70
CHI. I care not, I, knew she and all the world :
  I love Lavinia more than all the world.
DEM. Youngling, learn thou to make some meaner choice :
  Lavinia is thine elder brother's hope.
AAR. Why, are ye mad, or know ye not in Rome   75
  How furious and impatient they be,
  And cannot brook competitors in love ?
  I tell you, lords, you do but plot your deaths
  By this device.
CHI.   Aaron, a thousand deaths
  Would I propose to achieve her whom I love.   80
AAR. To achieve her—How ?
DEM. Why mak'st thou it so strange ?
  She is a woman, therefore may be woo'd ;
  She is a woman, therefore may be won ;
  She is Lavinia, therefore must be lov'd.
  What, man ! more water glideth by the mill   85
  Than wots the miller of ; and easy it is
  Of a cut loaf to steal a shive, we know.
  Though Bassianus be the Emperor's brother,
  Better than he have worn Vulcan's badge.
AAR. [*Aside.*] Ay, and as good as Saturninus may.   90
DEM. Then why should he despair that knows to court it
  With words, fair looks, and liberality ?
  What, hast not thou full often struck a doe,
  And borne her cleanly by the keeper's nose ?
AAR. Why, then, it seems some certain snatch or so   95

Marginal stage directions:

As they fight AARON knocks DEMETRIUS' legs from under him and brings them both down. *(at line 75)*

Line 90 spoken to camera. *(at line 90)*

    Would serve your turns.
CHI.   Ay, so the turn were served.
DEM. Aaron, thou hast hit it.
AAR.   Would you had hit it too !
    Then should not we be tir'd with this ado.
    Why, hark ye, hark ye ! and are you such fools
    To square for this ? Would it offend you, then,   100
    That both should speed ?
CHI. Faith, not me.
DEM.   Nor me, so I were one.
AAR. For shame, be friends, and join for that you jar.
    'Tis policy and stratagem must do
    That you affect ; and so must you resolve   105
    That what you cannot as you would achieve,
    You must perforce accomplish as you may.
    Take this of me : Lucrece was not more chaste
    Than this Lavinia, Bassianus' love.
    A speedier course than ling'ring languishment   110
    Must we pursue, and I have found the path.
    My lords, a solemn hunting is in hand ;
    There will the lovely Roman ladies troop ;
    The forest walks are wide and spacious,
    And many unfrequented plots there are   115
    Fitted by kind for rape and villainy.
    Single you thither then this dainty doe,
    And strike her home by force if not by words.
    This way, or not at all, stand you in hope.
    Come, come, our Empress, with her sacred wit   120
    To villainy and vengeance consecrate,
    Will we acquaint with all what we intend ;
    And she shall file our engines with advice
    That will not suffer you to square yourselves,
    But to your wishes' height advance you both.   125
    The Emperor's court is like the house of Fame,
    The palace full of tongues, of eyes, and ears ;
    The woods are ruthless, dreadful, deaf, and dull.
    There speak and strike, brave boys, and take your turns ;
    There serve your lust, shadowed from heaven's eye,   130
    And revel in Lavinia's treasury.
CHI. Thy counsel, lad, smells of no cowardice.
DEM. Sit fas aut nefas, till I find the stream
    To cool this heat, a charm to calm these fits,
    Per Styga, per manes vehor.   [*Exeunt.*

Latin spoken in English as 'Be it right or wrong'.

SCENE II.   *A forest near Rome.*

Enter TITUS ANDRONICUS, *and his three sons,* LUCIUS, QUINTUS, MARTIUS,
    making a noise with hounds and horns ; and MARCUS.

TIT. The hunt is up, the morn is bright and grey,
    The fields are fragrant, and the woods are green.
    Uncouple here, and let us make a bay,
    And wake the Emperor and his lovely bride,
    And rouse the Prince, and ring a hunter's peal,   5
    That all the court may echo with the noise.

SCENE 5
Rome. *Outside the Emperor's Palace.*

TITUS sends Y. LUCIUS off to give instructions to the hunters who are waiting outside the palace.

Sons, let it be your charge, as it is ours,
To attend the Emperor's person carefully.
I have been troubled in my sleep this night,
But dawning day new comfort hath inspir'd.   10

Here a cry of hounds, and wind horns in a peal.   *Then enter* SATURNINUS,
TAMORA, BASSIANUS, LAVINIA, CHIRON, DEMETRIUS, *and their*
ATTENDANTS.

Many good morrows to your Majesty !
Madam, to you as many and as good !
I promised your Grace a hunter's peal.
SAT. And you have rung it lustily, my lords—
Somewhat too early for new-married ladies.   15
BAS. Lavinia, how say you ?
LAV.   I say no ;
I have been broad awake two hours and more.
SAT. Come on then, horse and chariots let us have,
And to our sport. [*To Tamora.*]   Madam, now shall ye see
Our Roman hunting.
MARC.   I have dogs, my lord,   20
Will rouse the proudest panther in the chase,
And climb the highest promontory top.
TIT. And I have horse will follow where the game
Makes way, and run like swallows o'er the plain.
DEM. Chiron, we hunt not, we, with horse nor hound,   25
But hope to pluck a dainty doe to ground.   [*Exeunt.*

SCENE III.   *A lonely part of the forest.*

Enter AARON *alone, with a bag of gold.*

AAR. He that had wit would think that I had none,
To bury so much gold under a tree
And never after to inherit it.
Let him that thinks of me so abjectly
Know that this gold must coin a stratagem,   5
Which, cunningly effected, will beget
A very excellent piece of villainy.
And so repose, sweet gold, for their unrest   [*Hides the gold.*
That have their alms out of the Empress' chest.

Enter TAMORA *alone, to the Moor.*

TAM. My lovely Aaron, wherefore look'st thou sad   10
When everything doth make a gleeful boast ?
The birds chant melody on every bush ;
The snakes lie rolled in the cheerful sun ;
The green leaves quiver with the cooling wind.
And make a chequer'd shadow on the ground ;   15
Under their sweet shade, Aaron, let us sit,
And while the babbling echo mocks the hounds,
Replying shrilly to the well-tun'd horns,
As if a double hunt were heard at once,
Let us sit down and mark their yellowing noise ;   20
And—after conflict such as was suppos'd
The wand'ring prince and Dido once enjoyed,

Y. LUCIUS returns. The
hunters' peel is
sounding as trumpets
announce the arrival of
the Royal Party. TITUS
and his family greet
them formally.

Y. LUCIUS watches the
hunting party leave.

SCENE 6
A Clearing in the Forest.
There is a tree.

An arrow lands at
AARON's feet. He draws
a knife and turns to find
TAMORA with a bow in
her hands.

When with a happy storm they were surpris'd,
And curtain'd with a counsel-keeping cave—
We may, each wreathed in the other's arms,   25
Our pastimes done, possess a golden slumber,
Whiles hounds and horns and sweet melodious birds
Be unto us as is a nurse's song
Of lullaby to bring her babe asleep.
AAR. Madam, though Venus govern your desires,   30
Saturn is dominator over mine.
What signifies my deadly-standing eye,
My silence and my cloudy melancholy,
My fleece of woolly hair that now uncurls
Even as an adder when she doth unroll   35
To do some fatal execution ?
No, madam, these are no venereal signs.
Vengeance is in my heart, death in my hand,
Blood and revenge are hammering in my head.
Hark, Tamora, the empress of my soul,   40
Which never hopes more heaven than rests in thee—
This is the day of doom for Bassianus ;
His Philomel must lose her tongue to-day,
Thy sons make pillage of her chastity,
And wash their hands in Bassianus' blood.   45
Seest thou this letter ?   Take it up, I pray thee,
And give the King this fatal-plotted scroll.
Now question me no more ; we are espied.
Here comes a parcel of our hopeful booty,
Which dreads not yet their lives' destruction.   50

BASSIANUS and LAVINIA enter, but too far away to hear what is being said.

Enter BASSIANUS *and* LAVINIA.

TAM. Ah, my sweet Moor, sweeter to me than life !
AAR. No more, great Empress : Bassianus comes.
Be cross with him ; and I'll go fetch thy sons
To back thy quarrels, whatsoe'er they be.   [*Exit.*
BAS. Who have we here ?   Rome's royal Emperess,   55
Unfurnish'd of her well-beseeming troop ?
Or is it Dian, habited like her,
Who hath abandoned her holy groves
To see the general hunting in this forest ?
TAM. Saucy controller of my private steps !   60
Had I the pow'r that some say Dian had,
Thy temples should be planted presently
With horns, as was Actæon's ; and the hounds
Should drive upon thy new-transformed limbs,
Unmannerly intruder as thou art !   65
LAV. Under your patience, gentle Emperess,
'Tis thought you have a goodly gift in horning,
And to be doubted that your Moor and you
Are singled forth to try thy experiments.
Jove shield your husband from his hounds to-day !   70
'Tis pity they should take him for a stag.
BAS. Believe me, Queen, your swarth Cimmerian
Doth make your honour of his body's hue,
Spotted, detested, and abominable.

48

Why are you sequest'red from all your train,   75
Dismounted from your snow-white goodly steed,
And wand'red hither to an obscure plot,
Accompanied but with a barbarous Moor,
If foul desire had not conducted you?
LAV. And, being intercepted in your sport,   80
Great reason that my noble lord be rated
For sauciness. I pray you let us hence,
And let her joy her raven-coloured love;
This valley fits the purpose passing well.
BAS. The King my brother shall have notice of this.   85
LAV. Ay, for these slips have made him noted long.
Good king, to be so mightily abused!
TAM. Why, I have patience to endure all this.

Enter CHIRON *and* DEMETRIUS.

DEM. How now, dear sovereign, and our gracious mother!
Why doth your Highness look so pale and wan?   90
TAM. Have I not reason, think you, to look pale?
These two have 'ticed me hither to this place.
A barren detested vale you see it is:
The trees, though summer, yet forlorn and lean,
Overcome with moss and baleful mistletoe;   95
Here never shines the sun; here nothing breeds,
Unless the nightly owl or fatal raven.
And when they show'd me this abhorred pit,
They told me, here, at dead time of the night,
A thousand fiends, a thousand hissing snakes,   100
Ten thousand swelling toads, as many urchins,
Would make such fearful and confused cries
As any mortal body hearing it
Should straight fall mad or else die suddenly.
No sooner had they told this hellish tale   105
But straight they told me they would bind me here
Unto the body of a dismal yew,
And leave me to this miserable death.
And then they call'd me foul adulteress,
Lascivious Goth, and all the bitterest terms   110
That ever ear did hear to such effect;
And had you not by wondrous fortune come,
This vengeance on me had they executed.
Revenge it, as you love your mother's life,
Or be ye not henceforth call'd my children.   115
DEM. This is a witness that I am thy son.   [*Stabs Bassianus.*
CHI. And this for me, struck home to show my strength. [*Also stabs.*
LAV. Ay, come, Semiramis—nay, barbarous Tamora,
For no name fits thy nature but thy own!
TAM. Give me the poniard; you shall know, my boys,   120
Your mother's hand shall right your mother's wrong.
DEM. Stay, madam, here is more belongs to her;
First thrash the corn, then after burn the straw.
This minion stood upon her chastity,
Upon her nuptial vow, her loyalty,   125
And with that painted hope braves your mightiness;

TAMORA suddenly cries
out and sinks to the
ground. LAVINIA and
BASSIANUS turn to
watch her as CHIRON
and DEMETRIUS hurry
to their mother.

181

And shall she carry this unto her grave?
CHI. An if she do, I would I were an eunuch.
  Drag hence her husband to some secret hole,
  And make his dead trunk pillow to our lust.   130
TAM. But when ye have the honey we desire,
  Let not this wasp outlive, us both to sting.
CHI. I warrant you, madam, we will make that sure.
  Come, mistress, now perforce we will enjoy
  That nice-preserved honesty of yours.   135
LAV. O Tamora! thou bearest a woman's face—
TAM. I will not hear her speak; away with her!
LAV. Sweet lords, entreat her hear me but a word.
DEM. Listen, fair madam: let it be your glory
  To see her tears; but be your heart to them   140
  As unrelenting flint to drops of rain.
LAV. When did the tiger's young ones teach the dam?
  O, do not learn her wrath—she taught it thee;
  The milk thou suck'dst from her did turn to marble,
  Even at thy teat thou hadst thy tyranny.   145
  Yet every mother breeds not sons alike:
  [*To Chiron.*]   Do thou entreat her show a woman's pity.
CHI. What, wouldst thou have me prove myself a bastard?
LAV. 'Tis true, the raven doth not hatch a lark.
  Yet have I heard—O, could I find it now!—   150
  The lion, mov'd with pity, did endure
  To have his princely paws par'd all away.
  Some say that ravens foster forlorn children,
  The whilst their own birds famish in their nests;
  O, be to me, though thy hard heart say no,   155
  Nothing so kind, but something pitiful!
TAM. I know not what it means; away with her!
LAV. O, let me teach thee! For my father's sake,
  That gave thee life when well he might have slain thee,
  Be not obdurate, open thy deaf ears.   160
TAM. Hadst thou in person ne'er offended me,
  Even for his sake am I pitiless.
  Remember, boys, I pour'd forth tears in vain
  To save your brother from the sacrifice;
  But fierce Andronicus would not relent.   165
  Therefore away with her, and use her as you will;
  The worse to her the better lov'd of me.
LAV. O Tamora, be call'd a gentle queen,
  And with thine own hands kill me in this place!
  For 'tis not life that I have begg'd so long;   170
  Poor I was slain when Bassianus died.
TAM. What beg'st thou, then? Fond woman, let me go.
LAV. 'Tis present death I beg; and one thing more,
  That womanhood denies my tongue to tell:
  O, keep me from their worse than killing lust,   175
  And tumble me into some loathsome pit,
  Where never man's eye may behold my body;
  Do this, and be a charitable murderer.
TAM. So should I rob my sweet sons of their fee;
  No, let them satisfy their lust on thee.   180

DEM. Away ! for thou hast stay'd us here too long.
LAV. No grace ? no womanhood ? Ah, beastly creature,
   The blot and enemy to our general name !
   Confusion fall—
CHI. Nay, then I'll stop your mouth. Bring thou her husband. 185
   This is the hole where Aaron bid us hide him.

DEMETRIUS *throws the body of Bassianus into the pit; then exeunt*
      DEMETRIUS *and* CHIRON, *dragging off Lavinia.*

TAM. Farewell, my sons ; see that you make her sure.
   Ne'er let my heart know merry cheer indeed
   Till all the Andronici be made away.
   Now will I hence to seek my lovely Moor,   190
   And let my spleenful sons this trull deflower.   [*Exit.*

     Re-enter AARON, *with two of Titus' sons,*
        QUINTUS *and* MARTIUS.

AAR. Come on, my lords, the better foot before ;
   Straight will I bring you to the loathsome pit
   Where I espied the panther fast asleep.
QUIN. My sight is very dull, whate'er it bodes.   195
MART. And mine, I promise you ; were it not for shame,
   Well could I leave our sport to sleep awhile.   [*Falls into the pit.*
QUIN. What, art thou fallen ? What subtle hole is this,
   Whose mouth is covered with rude-growing briers,
   Upon whose leaves are drops of new-shed blood   200
   As fresh as morning dew distill'd on flowers ?
   A very fatal place it seems to me.
   Speak, brother, hast thou hurt thee with the fall ?
MART. O brother, with the dismal'st object hurt
   That ever eye with sight made heart lament !   205
AAR. [*Aside.*] Now will I fetch the King to find them here,
   That he thereby may have a likely guess
   How these were they that made away his brother.   [*Exit.*
MART. Why dost not comfort me, and help me out
   From this unhallow'd and blood-stained hole ?   210
QUIN. I am surprised with an uncouth fear ;
   A chilling sweat o'er-runs my trembling joints ;
   My heart suspects more than mine eye can see.
MART. To prove thou hast a true divining heart,
   Aaron and thou look down into this den,   215
   And see a fearful sight of blood and death.
QUIN. Aaron is gone, and my compassionate heart
   Will not permit mine eyes once to behold
   The thing whereat it trembles by surmise ;
   O, tell me who it is, for ne'er till now   220
   Was I a child to fear I know not what.
MART. Lord Bassianus lies beray'd in blood,
   All on a heap, like to a slaughtered lamb,
   In this detested, dark, blood-drinking pit.
QUIN. If it be dark, how dost thou know 'tis he ?   225
MART. Upon his bloody finger he doth wear
   A precious ring that lightens all this hole,
   Which, like a taper in some monument,

Lines 190–191 spoken to camera. AARON appears behind TAMORA during these lines.

Lines 206–208 spoken to camera.

Doth shine upon the dead man's earthy cheeks,
And shows the ragged entrails of this pit ;   230
So pale did shine the moon on Pyramus
When he by night lay bath'd in maiden blood.
O brother, help me with thy fainting hand—
If fear hath made thee faint, as me it hath—
Out of this fell devouring receptacle,   235
As hateful as Cocytus' misty mouth.
QUIN. Reach me thy hand, that I may help thee out,
Or, wanting strength to do thee so much good,
I may be pluck'd into the swallowing womb
Of this deep pit, poor Bassianus' grave.   240
I have no strength to pluck thee to the brink.
MART. Nor I no strength to climb without thy help.
QUIN. Thy hand once more ; I will not loose again,
Till thou art here aloft, or I below.
Thou canst not come to me—I come to thee.   [*Falls in.*

    Enter the EMPEROR *and* AARON *the Moor.*

SAT. Along with me ! I'll see what hole is here,   246
And what he is that now is leapt into it.
Say, who art thou that lately didst descend
Into this gaping hollow of the earth ?
MART. The unhappy sons of old Andronicus,   250
Brought hither in a most unlucky hour,
To find thy brother Bassianus dead.
SAT. My brother dead ! I know thou dost but jest :
He and his lady both are at the lodge
Upon the north side of this pleasant chase ;   255
'Tis not an hour since I left them there.
MART. We know not where you left them all alive ;
But, out alas ! here have we found him dead.

    Re-enter TAMORA, *with* ATTENDANTS ; TITUS   Soldiers accompany
    ANDRONICUS *and* LUCIUS.   TAMORA.

TAM. Where is my lord the King ?
SAT. Here, Tamora ; though griev'd with killing grief.   260
TAM. Where is thy brother Bassianus ?
SAT. Now to the bottom dost thou search my wound ;
Poor Bassianus here lies murdered.
TAM. Then all too late I bring this fatal writ,
The complot of this timeless tragedy ;   265
And wonder greatly that man's face can fold
In pleasing smiles such murderous tyranny.
                    [*She giveth Saturninus a letter.*
SAT. [*Reads.*] ' An if we miss to meet him handsomely,
Sweet huntsman—Bassianus 'tis we mean—
Do thou so much as dig the grave for him.   270
Thou know'st our meaning. Look for thy reward
Among the nettles at the elder-tree
Which overshades the mouth of that same pit
Where we decreed to bury Bassianus.
Do this, and purchase us thy lasting friends.'   275

Aaron (Hugh Quarshie) stands over the pit in which Quintus and Martius are trapped

Lavinia (Anna Calder-Marshall)
with Chiron (Michael Crompton)
and Demetrius (Neil McCaul)

O Tamora ! was ever heard the like ?
This is the pit and this the elder-tree.
Look, sirs, if you can find the huntsman out
That should have murdered Bassianus here.
AAR. My gracious lord, here is the bag of gold.   280
SAT. [*To* TITUS.]   Two of thy whelps, fell curs of bloody kind,
Have here bereft my brother of his life.
Sirs, drag them from the pit unto the prison ;
There let them bide until we have devis'd
Some never-heard-of torturing pain for them.   285
TAM. What, are they in this pit ?   O wondrous thing !
How easily murder is discovered !
TIT. High Emperor, upon my feeble knee
I beg this boon, with tears not lightly shed,
That this fell fault of my accursed sons—   290
Accursed if the fault be prov'd in them—
SAT. If it be prov'd !   You see it is apparent.
Who found this letter ?   Tamora, was it you ?
TAM. Andronicus himself did take it up.
TIT. I did, my lord, yet let me be their bail ;   295
For, by my fathers' reverend tomb, I vow
They shall be ready at your Highness' will
To answer their suspicion with their lives.
SAT. Thou shalt not bail them ; see thou follow me.
Some bring the murdered body, some the murderers ;   300
Let them not speak a word—the guilt is plain ;
For, by my soul, were there worse end than death,
That end upon them should be executed.
TAM. Andronicus, I will entreat the King.
Fear not thy sons ; they shall do well enough.   305
TIT. Come, Lucius, come ; stay not to talk with them.   [*Exeunt.*

SCENE IV.   *Another part of the forest.*

Enter the Empress' sons, DEMETRIUS *and* CHIRON, *with* LAVINIA, *her
hands cut off, and her tongue cut out, and ravish'd.*

DEM. So, now go tell, an if thy tongue can speak,
Who 'twas that cut thy tongue and ravish'd thee.
CHI. Write down thy mind, bewray thy meaning so,
An if thy stumps will let thee play the scribe.
DEM. See how with signs and tokens she can scrowl.   5
CHI. Go home, call for sweet water, wash thy hands.
DEM. She hath no tongue to call, nor hands to wash ;
And so let's leave her to her silent walks.
CHI. An 'twere my cause, I should go hang myself.
DEM. If thou hadst hands to help thee knit the cord.   10
                          [*Exeunt* DEMETRIUS *and* CHIRON.

Wind horns.   Enter MARCUS, *from hunting.*

MARC. Who is this ?—my niece, that flies away so fast ?
Cousin, a word : where is your husband ?
If I do dream, would all my wealth would wake me !
If I do wake, some planet strike me down,
That I may slumber an eternal sleep !   15

The soldiers move near
to the pit. They are
carrying a hoist.

The soldiers move to
the pit to set up the
hoist.

TITUS watches as his
sons are winched out of
the pit in a net. He
leaves but LUCIUS
watches. The boys hold
out their hands to him.

SCENE 7
*The same part of the
Forest.*

As CHIRON and
DEMETRIUS leave,
LAVINIA goes to the pit.

LAVINIA points to the
pit where she believes
BASSIANUS' body is.
MARCUS sees that she
has no hands.

Speak, gentle niece. What stern ungentle hands
Hath lopp'd, and hew'd, and made thy body bare
Of her two branches—those sweet ornaments
Whose circling shadows kings have sought to sleep in,
And might not gain so great a happiness   20
As half thy love ? Why dost not speak to me ?
Alas, a crimson river of warm blood,
Like to a bubbling fountain stirr'd with wind,
Doth rise and fall between thy rosed lips,
Coming and going with thy honey breath.   25
But sure some Tereus hath deflowered thee,
And, lest thou shouldst detect him, cut thy tongue.
Ah, now thou turn'st away thy face for shame !
And notwithstanding all this loss of blood—
As from a conduit with three issuing spouts—   30
Yet do thy cheeks look red as Titan's face
Blushing to be encount'red with a cloud.
Shall I speak for thee ? Shall I say 'tis so ?
O, that I knew thy heart, and knew the beast,
That I might rail at him to ease my mind !   35
Sorrow concealed, like an oven stopp'd,
Doth burn the heart to cinders where it is.
Fair Philomel, why she but lost her tongue,
And in a tedious sampler sew'd her mind ;
But, lovely niece, that mean is cut from thee.   40
A craftier Tereus, cousin, hast thou met,
And he hath cut those pretty fingers off
That could have better sew'd than Philomel.
O, had the monster seen those lily hands
Tremble like aspen leaves upon a lute   45
And make the silken strings delight to kiss them,
He would not then have touch'd them for his life !
Or had he heard the heavenly harmony
Which that sweet tongue hath made,
He would have dropp'd his knife, and fell asleep, 50
As Cerberus at the Thracian poet's feet.
Come, let us go, and make thy father blind,
For such a sight will blind a father's eye ;
One hour's storm will drown the fragrant meads,
What will whole months of tears thy father's eyes ? 55
Do not draw back, for we will mourn with thee ;
O, could our mourning ease thy misery !   [*Exeunt.*

LAVINIA, still in a state
of shock, realises as he
speaks that she has no
hands.

As LAVINIA tries to
speak she stares at the
blood which comes
from her mouth,
realising that she has
no tongue.

MARCUS takes LAVINIA
in his arms.

ACT THREE

SCENE I. *Rome. A street.*

Enter the JUDGES, TRIBUNES, *and* SENATORS, *with Titus' two sons*
MARTIUS *and* QUINTUS *bound, passing on the stage to the place of
execution, and* TITUS *going before, pleading.*

TIT. Hear me, grave fathers ; noble Tribunes, stay !
For pity of mine age, whose youth was spent
In dangerous wars whilst you securely slept ;
For all my blood in Rome's great quarrel shed,

SCENE 8
A Street in Rome.
Builders' ladders and
planks, tools and some
stones on a cart.

For all the frosty nights that I have watch'd,   5
And for these bitter tears, which now you see
Filling the aged wrinkles in my cheeks,
Be pitiful to my condemned sons,
Whose souls are not corrupted as 'tis thought.
For two and twenty sons I never wept,   10
Because they died in honour's lofty bed.   [ANDRONICUS *lieth*
     down, and the JUDGES *pass by him with the prisoners, and exeunt.*
For these, Tribunes, in the dust I write
My heart's deep languor and my soul's sad tears.
Let my tears stanch the earth's dry appetite ;
My sons' sweet blood will make it shame and blush.   15
O earth, I will befriend thee more with rain
That shall distil from these two ancient urns,
Than youthful April shall with all his show'rs.
In summer's drought I'll drop upon thee still ;
In winter with warm tears I'll melt the snow   20
And keep eternal spring-time on thy face,
So thou refuse to drink my dear sons' blood.

Enter LUCIUS *with his weapon drawn.*

O reverend Tribunes !   O gentle aged men !
Unbind my sons, reverse the doom of death,
And let me say, that never wept before,   25
My tears are now prevailing orators.
LUC. O noble father, you lament in vain ;
     The Tribunes hear you not, no man is by,
     And you recount your sorrows to a stone.
TIT. Ah, Lucius, for thy brothers let me plead !   30
     Grave Tribunes, once more I entreat of you.
LUC. My gracious lord, no tribune hears you speak.
TIT. Why, 'tis no matter, man : if they did hear,
     They would not mark me ; if they did mark,
     They would not pity me ; yet plead I must,   35
     And bootless unto them.
     Therefore I tell my sorrows to the stones ;   TITUS picks up a stone
     Who though they cannot answer my distress,   and holds it.
     Yet in some sort they are better than the Tribunes,
     For that they will not intercept my tale.   40
     When I do weep, they humbly at my feet
     Receive my tears, and seem to weep with me ;
     And were they but attired in grave weeds,
     Rome could afford no tribunes like to these.
     A stone is soft as wax : tribunes more hard than stones. 45
     A stone is silent and offendeth not,
     And tribunes with their tongues doom men to death.   [*Rises.*
     But wherefore stand'st thou with thy weapon drawn ?
LUC. To rescue my two brothers from their death ;
     For which attempt the judges have pronounc'd   50
     My everlasting doom of banishment.
TIT. O happy man ! they have befriended thee.
     Why, foolish Lucius, dost thou not perceive
     That Rome is but a wilderness of tigers ?

Tigers must prey, and Rome affords no prey   55
But me and mine ; how happy art thou then
From these devourers to be banished !
But who comes with our brother Marcus here ?

       Enter MARCUS *with* LAVINIA.   MARCUS enters with
                                                   LAVINIA hidden behind

MARC. Titus, prepare thy aged eyes to weep,
  Or if not so, thy noble heart to break.   60   him.
  I bring consuming sorrow to thine age.
TIT. Will it consume me ?   Let me see it then.
MARC. This was thy daughter.
TIT. Why, Marcus, so she is.
LUC. Ay me ! this object kills me.   LUCIUS collapses,
TIT. Faint-hearted boy, arise, and look upon her. 65   dropping his sword.
  Speak, Lavinia, what accursed hand   He is forced by TITUS to
  Hath made thee handless in thy father's sight ?   look at LAVINIA.
  What fool hath added water to the sea,
  Or brought a fagot to bright-burning Troy ?
  My grief was at the height before thou cam'st, 70
  And now like Nilus it disdaineth bounds.
  Give me a sword, I'll chop off my hands too,   TITUS is prevented by
  For they have fought for Rome, and all in vain ;   LUCIUS from using the
  And they have nurs'd this woe in feeding life ;   sword, which lies on
  In bootless prayer have they been held up,   75 the ground.
  And they have serv'd me to effectless use.
  Now all the service I require of them
  Is that the one will help to cut the other.
  'Tis well, Lavinia, that thou hast no hands ;
  For hands to do Rome service is but vain.   80
LUC. Speak, gentle sister, who hath martyr'd thee ?
MARC. O, that delightful engine of her thoughts
  That blabb'd them with such pleasing eloquence
  Is torn from forth that pretty hollow cage,
  Where like a sweet melodious bird it sung   85
  Sweet varied notes, enchanting every ear !
LUC. O, say thou for her, who hath done this deed ?
MARC. O, thus I found her straying in the park,
  Seeking to hide herself as doth the deer
  That hath receiv'd some unrecuring wound.   90
TIT. It was my dear, and he that wounded her
  Hath hurt me more than had he kill'd me dead ;
  For now I stand as one upon a rock,
  Environ'd with a wilderness of sea,
  Who marks the waxing tide grow wave by wave, 95
  Expecting ever when some envious surge
  Will in his brinish bowels swallow him.
  This way to death my wretched sons are gone ;
  Here stands my other son, a banish'd man,
  And here my brother, weeping at my woes.   100
  But that which gives my soul the greatest spurn
  Is dear Lavinia, dearer than my soul.
  Had I but seen thy picture in this plight,
  It would have madded me ; what shall I do
  Now I behold thy lively body so ?   105

Thou hast no hands to wipe away thy tears,
Nor tongue to tell me who hath martyr'd thee;
Thy husband he is dead, and for his death
Thy brothers are condemn'd, and dead by this.
Look, Marcus! Ah, son Lucius, look on her!   110
When I did name her brothers, then fresh tears
Stood on her cheeks, as doth the honey dew
Upon a gath'red lily almost withered.

MARC. Perchance she weeps because they kill'd her husband;
    Perchance because she knows them innocent.   115

TIT. If they did kill thy husband, then be joyful,
    Because the law hath ta'en revenge on them.
    No, no, they would not do so foul a deed;
    Witness the sorrow that their sister makes.

    Gentle Lavinia, let me kiss thy lips,   120   *LAVINIA leaves them*
    Or make some sign how I may do thee ease.   *and sits. They gather*
    Shall thy good uncle and thy brother Lucius   *round her.*
    And thou and I sit round about some fountain,
    Looking all downwards to behold our cheeks
    How they are stain'd, like meadows yet not dry   125
    With miry slime left on them by a flood?
    And in the fountain shall we gaze so long,
    Till the fresh taste be taken from that clearness,
    And made a brine-pit with our bitter tears?
    Or shall we cut away our hands like thine?   130
    Or shall we bite our tongues, and in dumb shows
    Pass the remainder of our hateful days?
    What shall we do? Let us that have our tongues
    Plot some device of further misery
    To make us wonder'd at in time to come.   135

LUC. Sweet father, cease your tears; for at your grief
    See how my wretched sister sobs and weeps.

MARC. Patience, dear niece. Good Titus, dry thine eyes.

TIT. Ah, Marcus, Marcus! Brother, well I wot
    Thy napkin cannot drink a tear of mine,   140
    For thou, poor man, hast drown'd it with thine own.

LUC. Ah, my Lavinia, I will wipe thy cheeks.

TIT. Mark, Marcus, mark! I understand her signs.
    Had she a tongue to speak, now would she say
    That to her brother which I said to thee: 145
    His napkin, with his true tears all bewet,
    Can do no service on her sorrowful cheeks.
    O, what a sympathy of woe is this—
    As far from help as Limbo is from bliss!

            Enter AARON *the Moor.*

AAR. Titus Andronicus, my lord the Emperor   150
    Sends thee this word, that, if thou love thy sons,
    Let Marcus, Lucius, or thyself, old Titus,
    Or any one of you, chop off your hand
    And send it to the King: he for the same
    Will send thee hither both thy sons alive,   155
    And that shall be the ransom for their fault.

TIT. O gracious Emperor! O gentle Aaron!

Did ever raven sing so like a lark
That gives sweet tidings of the sun's uprise ?
With all my heart I'll send the Emperor my hand.   260
Good Aaron, wilt thou help to chop it off ?
LUC. Stay, father ! for that noble hand of thine,
That hath thrown down so many enemies,
Shall not be sent.   My hand will serve the turn,
My youth can better spare my blood than you,
And therefore mine shall save my brothers' lives.
MARC. Which of your hands hath not defended Rome
And rear'd aloft the bloody battle-axe,
Writing destruction on the enemy's castle ?   170
O, none of both but are of high desert !
My hand hath been but idle ; let it serve
To ransom my two nephews from their death ;
Then have I kept it to a worthy end.
AAR. Nay, come, agree whose hand shall go along,   175
For fear they die before their pardon come.
MARC. My hand shall go.
LUC.   By heaven, it shall not go !
TIT. Sirs, strive no more ; such with'red herbs as these
Are meet for plucking up, and therefore mine.
LUC. Sweet father, if I shall be thought thy son,   180
Let me redeem my brothers both from death.
MARC. And for our father's sake and mother's care,
Now let me show a brother's love to thee.
TIT. Agree between you ; I will spare my hand.
LUC. Then I'll go fetch an axe.   185
MARC. But I will use the axe.   [*Exeunt* LUCIUS *and* MARCUS.
TIT. Come hither, Aaron, I'll deceive them both ;
Lend me thy hand, and I will give thee mine.
| AAR. [*Aside.*]   If that be call'd deceit, I will be honest,
| And never whilst I live deceive men so ;   190 |
| But I'll deceive you in another sort,
| And that you'll say ere half an hour pass.
                              [*He cuts off Titus' hand.*

                Re-enter LUCIUS *and* MARCUS.

TIT. Now stay your strife.   What shall be is dispatch'd.
Good Aaron, give his Majesty my hand ;
Tell him it was a hand that warded him   195
From thousand dangers ; bid him bury it.
More hath it merited—that let it have.
As for my sons, say I account of them
As jewels purchas'd at an easy price ;
And yet dear too, because I bought mine own.   200
AAR. I go, Andronicus ; and for thy hand
Look by and by to have thy sons with thee.
| [*Aside.*]   Their heads I mean.   O, how this villainy
| Doth fat me with the very thoughts of it !
| Let fools do good, and fair men call for grace :   205 |
| Aaron will have his soul black like his face.   [*Exit.* |
TIT. O, here I lift this one hand up to heaven,
And bow this feeble ruin to the earth ;

LUCIUS and MARCUS
fight over an axe which
is among the builders'
tools.

Lines 189–192 spoken
to camera.

Lines 203–206 spoken
to camera.

If any power pities wretched tears,
To that I call ! [*To* LAVINIA.] What, would'st thou kneel with me ?
Do, then, dear heart ; for heaven shall hear our prayers,   211
Or with our sighs we'll breathe the welkin dim
And stain the sun with fog, as sometime clouds
When they do hug him in their melting bosoms.

MARC. O brother, speak with possibility,   215
And do not break into these deep extremes.

TIT. Is not my sorrow deep, having no bottom ?
Then be my passions bottomless with them.

MARC. But yet let reason govern thy lament.

TIT. If there were reason for these miseries,   220
Then into limits could I bind my woes.
When heaven doth weep, doth not the earth o'erflow ?
If the winds rage, doth not the sea wax mad,
Threat'ning the welkin with his big-swol'n face ?
And wilt thou have a reason for this coil ?   225
I am the sea ; hark how her sighs do blow.
She is the weeping welkin, I the earth ;
Then must my sea be moved with her sighs ;
Then must my earth with her continual tears
Become a deluge, overflow'd and drown'd ;   230
For why my bowels cannot hide her woes,
But like a drunkard must I vomit them.
Then give me leave ; for losers will have leave
To ease their stomachs with their bitter tongues.

Enter a MESSENGER, *with two heads and a hand.*

MESS. Worthy Andronicus, ill art thou repaid   235
For that good hand thou sent'st the Emperor.
Here are the heads of thy two noble sons ;
And here's thy hand, in scorn to thee sent back-
Thy grief their sports, thy resolution mock'd,
That woe is me to think upon thy woes,   240
More than remembrance of my father's death.   [*Exit.*

MARC. Now let hot Ætna cool in Sicily,
And be my heart an ever-burning hell !
These miseries are more than may be borne.
To weep with them that weep doth ease some deal,   245
But sorrow flouted at is double death.

LUC. Ah, that this sight should make so deep a wound,
And yet detested life not shrink thereat !
That ever death should let life bear his name,
Where life hath no more interest but to breathe !   250
                    [LAVINIA *kisses Titus.*

MARC. Alas, poor heart, that kiss is comfortless
As frozen water to a starved snake.

TIT. When will this fearful slumber have an end ?

MARC. Now farewell, flatt'ry ; die, Andronicus.
Thou dost not slumber : see thy two sons' heads,   255
Thy warlike hand, thy mangled daughter here ;
Thy other banish'd son with this dear sight
Struck pale and bloodless ; and thy brother, I,
Even like a stony image, cold and numb.

                    ·

The Messenger carries the heads and hand in a basket covered with a white cloth.

LUCIUS removes the white cloth.

Ah ! now no more will I control thy griefs.   260
Rent off thy silver hair, thy other hand
Gnawing with thy teeth ; and be this dismal sight
The closing up of our most wretched eyes.
Now is a time to storm ; why art thou still ?
TIT. Ha, ha, ha !   265
MARC. Why dost thou laugh ?   It fits not with this hour.
TIT. Why, I have not another tear to shed ;
Besides, this sorrow is an enemy,
And would usurp upon my wat'ry eyes
And make them blind with tributary tears.   270
Then which way shall I find Revenge's cave ?
For these two heads do seem to speak to me,
And threat me I shall never come to bliss
Till all these mischiefs be return'd again
Even in their throats that have committed them.   275
Come, let me see what task I have to do.
You heavy people, circle me about,
That I may turn me to each one of you
And swear unto my soul to right your wrongs.   As they stand in a circle
The vow is made.   Come, brother, take a head,   280   TITUS moves to each of
And in this hand the other will I bear.   them in turn and looks
And, Lavinia, thou shalt be employ'd in this ;   at them.
Bear thou my hand, sweet wench, between thy teeth.
As for thee, boy, go, get thee from my sight ;
Thou art an exile, and thou must not stay.   285
Hie to the Goths and raise an army there ;
And if ye love me, as I think you do,
Let's kiss and part, for we have much to do.
                                        [*Exeunt all but Lucius.*
LUC. Farewell, Andronicus, my noble father,
The woefull'st man that ever liv'd in Rome.   290
Farewell, proud Rome ; till Lucius come again,
He leaves his pledges dearer than his life.
Farewell, Lavinia, my noble sister ;
O, would thou wert as thou tofore hast been !
But now nor Lucius nor Lavinia lives   295
But in oblivion and hateful griefs.
If Lucius live, he will requite your wrongs
And make proud Saturnine and his emperess
Beg at the gates like Tarquin and his queen.
Now will I to the Goths, and raise a pow'r   300 | Lines 300–301 spoken
To be reveng'd on Rome and Saturnine.   [*Exit.* | to camera.

SCENE II.   *Rome.   Titus' house.*

A banquet.   Enter TITUS, MARCUS, LAVINIA,   SCENE 9
and the boy YOUNG LUCIUS.   *Titus' House.*
                                                               Three servants wait to
TIT. So so, now sit ; and look you eat no more   serve a simple meal.
Than will preserve just so much strength in us   Y. LUCIUS is reading a
As will revenge these bitter woes of ours.   book. He looks up to
Marcus, unknit that sorrow-wreathen knot ;   see TITUS, LAVINIA and
Thy niece and I, poor creatures, want our hands,   5   MARCUS coming
And cannot passionate our tenfold grief   towards him.

With folded arms. This poor right hand of mine
Is left to tyrannize upon my breast;
Who, when my heart, all mad with misery,
Beats in this hollow prison of my flesh,   10
Then thus I thump it down.
[*To* LAVINIA.] Thou map of woe, that thus dost talk in signs !
When thy poor heart beats with outrageous beating,
Thou canst not strike it thus to make it still.
Wound it with sighing, girl, kill it with groans;   15
Or get some little knife between thy teeth
And just against thy heart make thou a hole,
That all the tears that thy poor eyes let fall
May run into that sink and, soaking in,
Drown the lamenting fool in sea-salt tears.   20
MARC. Fie, brother, fie ! Teach her not thus to lay
Such violent hands upon her tender life.
TIT. How now ! Has sorrow made thee dote already ?
Why, Marcus, no man should be mad but I.
What violent hands can she lay on her life ?   25
Ah, wherefore dost thou urge the name of hands ?
To bid Æneas tell the tale twice o'er
How Troy was burnt and he made miserable ?
O, handle not the theme, to talk of hands,
Lest we remember still that we have none.   30
Fie, fie, how franticly I square my talk,
As if we should forget we had no hands,
If Marcus did not name the word of hands !
Come, let's fall to; and, gentle girl, eat this :
Here is no drink. Hark, Marcus, what she says—   35
I can interpret all her martyr'd signs;
She says she drinks no other drink but tears,
Brew'd with her sorrow, mesh'd upon her cheeks.
Speechless complainer, I will learn thy thought;
In thy dumb action will I be as perfect   40
As begging hermits in their holy prayers.
Thou shalt not sigh, nor hold thy stumps to heaven,
Nor wink, nor nod, nor kneel, nor make a sign,
But I of these will wrest an alphabet,
And by still practice learn to know thy meaning.   45
BOY. Good grandsire, leave these bitter deep laments;
Make my aunt merry with some pleasing tale.
MARC. Alas, the tender boy, in passion mov'd,
Doth weep to see his grandsire's heaviness.
TIT. Peace, tender sapling; thou art made of tears,   50
And tears will quickly melt thy life away.
                [MARCUS *strikes the dish with a knife.*
What dost thou strike at, Marcus, with thy knife ?
MARC. At that that I have kill'd, my lord—a fly.
TIT. Out on thee, murderer, thou kill'st my heart !
Mine eyes are cloy'd with view of tyranny;   55
A deed of death done on the innocent
Becomes not Titus' brother. Get thee gone;
I see thou art not for my company.
MARC. Alas, my lord, I have but kill'd a fly.

LAVINIA tries to express
something to MARCUS,
using her handless
arms.

Lines 26–28 omitted.

TITUS feeds LAVINIA
with a spoon. She
rejects the food. As he
shouts at the servant
for drink, LAVINIA
again tries to express
something.

TITUS moves to
embrace YOUNG
LUCIUS.

TIT. ' But ' !   How if that fly had a father and mother ?   60
How would he hang his slender gilded wings
And buzz lamenting doings in the air !
Poor harmless fly,
That with his pretty buzzing melody
Came here to make us merry !   And thou hast kill'd him.
MARC. Pardon me, sir ; it was a black ill-favour'd fly,   66
Like to the Empress' Moor ; therefore I kill'd him.
TIT. O, O, O !
Then pardon me for reprehending thee,
For thou hast done a charitable deed.   70
Give me thy knife, I will insult on him,
Flattering myself as if it were the Moor
Come hither purposely to poison me.
There's for thyself, and that's for Tamora.
Ah, sirrah !   75
Yet, I think, we are not brought so low
But that between us we can kill a fly
That comes in likeness of a coal-black Moor.
MARC. Alas, poor man ! grief has so wrought on him,
He takes false shadows for true substances.   80
TIT. Come, take away.   Lavinia, go with me ;
I'll to thy closet, and go read with thee
Sad stories chanced in the times of old.
Come, boy, and go with me ; thy sight is young,
And thou shalt read when mine begin to dazzle.   [*Exeunt.*

TITUS demands a knife
from YOUNG LUCIUS.

MARCUS is left alone at
the table.

ACT FOUR

SCENE I.   *Rome.   Titus' garden.*

Enter YOUNG LUCIUS *and* LAVINIA *running after him, and the boy flies
from her with his books under his arm.   Enter* TITUS *and* MARCUS.

BOY. Help, grandsire, help ! my aunt Lavinia
Follows me everywhere, I know not why.
Good uncle Marcus, see how swift she comes !
Alas, sweet aunt, I know not what you mean.
MARC. Stand by me, Lucius ; do not fear thine aunt.   5
TIT. She loves thee, boy, too well to do thee harm.
BOY. Ay, when my father was in Rome she did.
MARC. What means my niece Lavinia by these signs ?
TIT. Fear her not, Lucius ; somewhat doth she mean.
See, Lucius, see how much she makes of thee.   10
Somewhither would she have thee go with her.
Ah, boy, Cornelia never with more care
Read to her sons than she hath read to thee
Sweet poetry and Tully's Orator.
MARC. Canst thou not guess wherefore she plies thee thus ?   15
BOY. My lord, I know not, I, nor can I guess,
Unless some fit or frenzy do possess her ;
For I have heard my grandsire say full oft
Extremity of griefs would make men mad ;
And I have read that Hecuba of Troy   20
Ran mad for sorrow.   That made me to fear ;

SCENE 10
*The Garden of Titus'
House.*

A series of images
showing LAVINIA
chasing YOUNG LUCIUS,
who drops his school
books in his panic.

Although, my lord, I know my noble aunt
Loves me as dear as e'er my mother did,
And would not, but in fury, fright my youth ;
Which made me down to throw my books, and fly—   25
Causeless, perhaps.   But pardon me, sweet aunt ;
And, madam, if my uncle Marcus go,
I will most willingly attend your ladyship.
MARC. Lucius, I will.   [LAVINIA *turns over with her stumps the books*   LAVINIA leads them to
                                  which LUCIUS *has let fall.*   where the school books
TIT. How now, Lavinia !   Marcus, what means this ?   30   lie on the ground.
Some book there is that she desires to see.
Which is it, girl, of these ?—Open them, boy.—
But thou art deeper read and better skill'd ;
Come and take choice of all my library,
And so beguile thy sorrow, till the heavens   35
Reveal the damn'd contriver of this deed.
Why lifts she up her arms in sequence thus ?
MARC. I think she means that there were more than one
Confederate in the fact ; ay, more there was,
Or else to heaven she heaves them for revenge.   40
TIT. Lucius, what book is that she tosseth so ?
BOY. Grandsire, 'tis Ovid's Metamorphoses ;
My mother gave it me.
MARC.   For love of her that's gone,
Perhaps she cull'd it from among the rest.
TIT. Soft !   So busily she turns the leaves !   Help her.   45
What would she find ?   Lavinia, shall I read ?
This is the tragic tale of Philomel
And treats of Tereus' treason and his rape ;
And rape, I fear, was root of thy annoy.
MARC. See, brother, see !   Note how she quotes the leaves.
TIT. Lavinia, wert thou thus surpris'd, sweet girl,
Ravish'd and wrong'd as Philomela was,
Forc'd in the ruthless, vast, and gloomy woods ?
See, see !   55   LAVINIA shows TITUS a
Ay, such a place there is where we did hunt—   picture of woods.
O, had we never, never hunted there !—
Pattern'd by that the poet here describes,
By nature made for murders and for rapes.
MARC. O, why should nature build so foul a den,   60
Unless the gods delight in tragedies ?
TIT. Give signs, sweet girl, for here are none but friends,
What Roman lord it was durst do the deed.
Or slunk not Saturnine, as Tarquin erst,   TITUS shakes LAVINIA
That left the camp to sin in Lucrece' bed ?   65   roughly. She cries out
MARC. Sit down, sweet niece ;   brother, sit down by me.   in terror – a strange
Apollo, Pallas, Jove, or Mercury,   rasping sound.
Inspire me, that I may this treason find !
My lord, look here !   Look here, Lavinia !   [*He writes his name*   MARCUS writes in the
                    with his staff, and guides it with feet and mouth.   sand with Titus' staff,
This sandy plot is plain ;   guide, if thou canst.   70   which he holds in his
This after me.   I have writ my name   arms without using his
Without the help of any hand at all.   hands.
Curs'd be that heart that forc'd us to this shift !

Write thou, good niece, and here display at last
What God will have discovered for revenge.					75
Heaven guide thy pen to print thy sorrows plain,
That we may know the traitors and the truth ! [*She takes the*
     staff in her mouth and guides it with her stumps, and writes.
O, do ye read, my lord, what she hath writ ?
TIT. ' Stuprum—Chiron—Demetrius.'
MARC. What, what ! the lustful sons of Tamora					80
Performers of this heinous bloody deed ?
TIT. Magni Dominator poli,
Tam lentus audis scelera ? tam lentus vides ?
MARC. O, calm thee, gentle lord ! although I know
There is enough written upon this earth					85
To stir a mutiny in the mildest thoughts,
And arm the minds of infants to exclaims.
My lord, kneel down with me ; Lavinia, kneel ;
And kneel, sweet boy, the Roman Hector's hope ;
And swear with me—as, with the woeful fere					90
And father of that chaste dishonoured dame,
Lord Junius Brutus sware for Lucrece' rape—
That we will prosecute, by good advice,
Mortal revenge upon these traitorous Goths,
And see their blood or die with this reproach.					95
TIT. 'Tis sure enough, an you knew how ;
But if you hunt these bear-whelps, then beware :
The dam will wake ; and if she wind ye once,
She's with the lion deeply still in league,
And lulls him whilst she playeth on her back,					100
And when he sleeps will she do what she list.
You are a young huntsman, Marcus ; let alone ;
And come, I will go get a leaf of brass,
And with a gad of steel will write these words,
And lay it by. The angry northern wind					105
Will blow these sands like Sibyl's leaves abroad,
And where's our lesson, then ? Boy, what say you ?
BOY. I say, my lord, that if I were a man
Their mother's bedchamber should not be safe
For these base bondmen to the yoke of Rome.					110
MARC. Ay, that's my boy ! Thy father hath full oft
For his ungrateful country done the like.
BOY. And, uncle, so will I, an if I live.
TIT. Come, go with me into mine armoury.
Lucius, I'll fit thee ; and withal my boy					115
Shall carry from me to the Empress' sons
Presents that I intend to send them both.
Come, come ; thou'lt do my message, wilt thou not ?
BOY. Ay, with my dagger in their bosoms, grandsire.
TIT. No, boy, not so ; I'll teach thee another course.					120
Lavinia, come. Marcus, look to my house.
Lucius and I'll go brave it at the court ;
Ay, marry, will we, sir ! and we'll be waited on. [*Exeunt* TITUS,
     LAVINIA, *and* YOUNG LUCIUS.
MARC. O heavens, can you hear a good man groan
And not relent, or not compassion him ?					125

TITUS and MARCUS move away as LAVINIA begins to write. When she has finished she passes the staff to YOUNG LUCIUS who has watched her, and goes to kneel at Titus' feet. Line 79: for 'Stuprum' read 'Rape'. Lines 80–81 omitted.

TITUS throws a handful of sand.

Y. LUCIUS draws his dagger. It is the one with which TITUS killed MUTIUS.

LAVINIA does not exit.

Marcus, attend him in his ecstasy,
That hath more scars of sorrow in his heart
Than foemen's marks upon his batt'red shield,
But yet so just that he will not revenge.
Revenge the heavens for old Andronicus!   [*Exit.*

Lines 127–130 spoken
to camera.

After MARCUS' exit
LAVINIA rubs out the
writing in the sand.

SCENE II. *Rome. The palace.*

Enter AARON, DEMETRIUS *and* CHIRON, *at one door ; and at the other
door,* YOUNG LUCIUS *and* ANOTHER *with a bundle of weapons, and
verses writ upon them.*

SCENE II
*A Room in the
Emperor's Palace.*
CHIRON and DEMETRIUS
are throwing food at
each other. AARON sits
at the end of the table.
He notices Y. LUCIUS
and PUBLIUS
approaching.

CHI. Demetrius, here's the son of Lucius ;
    He hath some message to deliver us.
AAR. Ay, some mad message from his mad grandfather.
BOY. My lords, with all the humbleness I may,
    I greet your honours from Andronicus—   5
    [*Aside.*] And pray the Roman gods confound you both !
DEM. Gramercy, lovely Lucius.   What's the news ?
BOY. [*Aside.*]   That you are both decipher'd, that's the news,
    For villains mark'd with rape.—May it please you,
    My grandsire, well-advis'd, hath sent by me   10
    The goodliest weapons of his armoury
    To gratify your honourable youth,
    The hope of Rome ; for so he bid me say ;
    And so I do, and with his gifts present
    Your lordships, that, whenever you have need,   15
    You may be armed and appointed well.
    And so I leave you both—[*Aside.*] like bloody villains.
              [*Exeunt* YOUNG LUCIUS *and* ATTENDANT.
DEM. What's here ?   A scroll, and written round about.
    Let's see :
    [*Reads.*] ' Integer vitae, scelerisque purus,   20
    Non eget Mauri iaculis, nec arcu.'
CHI. O, 'tis a verse in Horace, I know it well ;
    I read it in the grammar long ago.
AAR. Ay, just—a verse in Horace.   Right, you have it.
    [*Aside.*]   Now, what a thing it is to be an ass !   25
    Here's no sound jest !   The old man hath found their guilt,
    And sends them weapons wrapp'd about with lines
    That wound, beyond their feeling, to the quick.
    But were our witty Empress well afoot,
    She would applaud Andronicus' conceit.   30
    But let her rest in her unrest awhile—
    And now, young lords, was't not a happy star
    Led us to Rome, strangers, and more than so,
    Captives, to be advanced to this height ?
    It did me good before the palace gate   35
    To brave the Tribune in his brother's hearing.
DEM. But me more good to see so great a lord
    Basely insinuate and send us gifts.
AAR. Had he not reason, Lord Demetrius ?
    Did you not use his daughter very friendly ?   40

Line 6 spoken to
camera.
Lines 8–9, '. . . mark'd
with rape', spoken to
camera.

For 'his' read 'these'.

'Like bloody villains'
spoken to camera.

Lines 25–31 spoken to
camera.

DEM. I would we had a thousand Roman dames
  At such a bay, by turn to serve our lust.
CHI. A charitable wish and full of love.
AAR. Here lacks but your mother for to say amen.
CHI. And that would she for twenty thousand more.   45
DEM. Come, let us go and pray to all the gods
  For our beloved mother in her pains.
AAR. [*Aside.*]   Pray to the devils ; the gods have given us over.
                                                  [*Trumpets sound.*
DEM. Why do the Emperor's trumpets flourish thus ?
CHI. Belike, for joy the Emperor hath a son.   50
DEM. Soft ! who comes here ?

            Enter NURSE, *with a blackamoor* CHILD.

NUR. Good morrow, lords.
  O, tell me, did you see Aaron the Moor ?
AAR. Well, more or less, or ne'er a whit at all,
  Here Aaron is ; and what with Aaron now ?
NUR. O gentle Aaron, we are all undone !   55
  Now help, or woe betide thee evermore !
AAR. Why, what a caterwauling dost thou keep !
  What dost thou wrap and fumble in thy arms ?
NUR. O, that which I would hide from heaven's eye :
  Our Empress' shame and stately Rome's disgrace !   60
  She is delivered, lords ; she is delivered.
AAR. To whom ?
NUR.   I mean she is brought a-bed.
AAR. Well, God give her good rest !   What hath he sent her ?
NUR. A devil.
AAR.   Why, then she is the devil's dam ;
  A joyful issue.   65
NUR. A joyless, dismal, black, and sorrowful issue !
  Here is the babe, as loathsome as a toad
  Amongst the fair-fac'd breeders of our clime ;
  The Empress sends it thee, thy stamp, thy seal,
  And bids thee christen it with thy dagger's point.   70
AAR. Zounds, ye whore !   Is black so base a hue ?
  Sweet blowse, you are a beauteous blossom sure.
DEM. Villain, what hast thou done ?
AAR. That which thou canst not undo.
CHI. Thou hast undone our mother.   75
AAR. Villain, I have done thy mother.
DEM. And therein, hellish dog, thou hast undone her.
  Woe to her chance, and damn'd her loathed choice !
  Accurs'd the offspring of so foul a fiend !
CHI. It shall not live.   80
AAR. It shall not die.
NUR. Aaron, it must ; the mother wills it so.
AAR. What, must it, nurse ?   Then let no man but I
  Do execution on my flesh and blood.
DEM. I'll broach the tadpole on my rapier's point.   85
  Nurse, give it me ; my sword shall soon dispatch it.
AAR. Sooner this sword shall plough thy bowels up.   [*Takes the
                                  Child from the Nurse, and draws.*

The NURSE enters
carrying a bundle not
immediately
recognisable as a baby.

The NURSE lays the
baby on the table.
AARON unwraps it.

The NURSE picks up the
baby as AARON
suddenly draws a
sword.

Stay, murderous villains, will you kill your brother !
Now, by the burning tapers of the sky
That shone so brightly when this boy was got,   90
He dies upon my scimitar's sharp point
That touches this my first-born son and heir.
I tell you, younglings, not Enceladus,
With all his threat'ning band of Typhon's brood,
Nor great Alcides, nor the god of war,   95
Shall seize this prey out of his father's hands.
What, what, ye sanguine, shallow-hearted boys !
Ye white-lim'd walls ! ye alehouse painted signs !
Coal-black is better than another hue
In that it scorns to bear another hue ;   100
For all the water in the ocean
Can never turn the swan's black legs to white,
Although she lave them hourly in the flood.
Tell the Empress from me I am of age   AARON takes the baby
To keep mine own—excuse it how she can.   105   from the NURSE.
DEM. Wilt thou betray thy noble mistress thus ?
AAR. My mistress is my mistress : this my self,
      The vigour and the picture of my youth.
      This before all the world do I prefer ;
      This maugre all the world will I keep safe,   110
      Or some of you shall smoke for it in Rome.
DEM. By this our mother is for ever sham'd.
CHI. Rome will despise her for this foul escape.
NUR. The Emperor in his rage will doom her death.
CHI. I blush to think upon this ignomy.   115
AAR. Why, there's the privilege your beauty bears :
      Fie, treacherous hue, that will betray with blushing
      The close enacts and counsels of thy heart !
      Here's a young lad fram'd of another leer.
      Look how the black slave smiles upon the father,   120
      As who should say ' Old lad, I am thine own '.
      He is your brother, lords, sensibly fed
      Of that self-blood that first gave life to you ;
      And from your womb where you imprisoned were
      He is enfranchised and come to light.   125
      Nay, he is your brother by the surer side,
      Although my seal be stamped in his face.
NUR. Aaron, what shall I say unto the Empress ?
DEM. Advise thee, Aaron, what is to be done,
      And we will all subscribe to thy advice.   130
      Save thou the child, so we may all be safe.
AAR. Then sit we down and let us all consult.
      My son and I will have the wind of you :
      Keep there ; now talk at pleasure of your safety.   [They sit.
DEM. How many women saw this child of his ?   135
AAR. Why, so, brave lords ! When we join in league
      I am a lamb ; but if you brave the Moor,
      The chafed boar, the mountain lioness,
      The ocean swells not so as Aaron storms.
      But say, again, how many saw the child ?   140
NUR. Cornelia the midwife and myself ;

*Tamora (Eileen Atkins) pleads with Titus (Trevor Peacock) for the life of her son Alarbus
(Peter Searles). Young Lucius (Paul Davies-Prowles) looks on. Behind Tamora,
Chiron and Aaron can be seen*

*Chiron (Michael Crompton), Aaron (Hugh
Quarshie), Demetrius (Neil McCaul)
and Tamora*

Hugh Quarshie as Aaron

Lavinia (Anna Calder-Marshall) pleads with Tamora (Eileen Atkins), watched by Demetrius (Neil McCaul) and Chiron (Michael Crompton)

Young Lucius (Paul Davies-Prowles), Lavinia and Titus (Trevor Peacock)

Aaron (Hugh Quarshie) cuts off Titus' hand

Lavinia writes in the sand, watched by Young Lucius

Chiron, Demetrius and Tamora as Rape, Murder and Revenge

Lucius (Gavin Richards, back to camera), Tamora (Eileen Atkins), Saturninus (Brian Protheroe), Aemilius (Walter Brown) and Titus (Trevor Peacock)

Lucius (Gavin Richards), Young Lucius (Paul Davies-Prowles) and Marcus (Edward Hardwicke) with the body of Titus

And no one else but the delivered Empress.
AAR. The Emperess, the midwife, and yourself.
Two may keep counsel when the third's away :
Go to the Empress, tell her this I said.   [*He kills her.*   AARON stabs the NURSE
Weeke weeke !   146   with a dagger.
So cries a pig prepared to the spit.
DEM. What mean'st thou, Aaron ? Wherefore didst thou this ?
AAR. O Lord, sir, 'tis a deed of policy.
Shall she live to betray this guilt of ours—   150
A long-tongu'd babbling gossip ?   No, lords, no.
And now be it known to you my full intent :
Not far, one Muliteus, my countryman—
His wife but yesternight was brought to bed ;
His child is like to her, fair as you are.   155
Go pack with him, and give them the mother gold,
And tell them both the circumstance of all,
And how by this their child shall be advanc'd,
And be received for the Emperor's heir
And substituted in the place of mine,   160
To calm this tempest whirling in the court ;
And let the Emperor dandle him for his own.
Hark ye, lords.   You see I have given her physic, [*Pointing to
                                                     the Nurse.*
And you must needs bestow her funeral ;
The fields are near, and you are gallant grooms.   165
This done, see that you take no longer days,
But send the midwife presently to me.
The midwife and the nurse well made away,
Then let the ladies tattle what they please.
CHI. Aaron, I see thou wilt not trust the air   170
With secrets.
DEM.   For this care of Tamora,
Herself and hers are highly bound to thee.   [*Exeunt* DEMETRIUS
                                      and CHIRON, *bearing off the dead Nurse.*
AAR. Now to the Goths, as swift as swallow flies, | Lines 173–175 spoken
There to dispose this treasure in mine arms, | to camera.
And secretly to greet the Empress' friends.   175 |
Come on, you thick-lipp'd slave, I'll bear you hence ;
For it is you that puts us to our shifts.
I'll make you feed on berries and on roots,
And feed on curds and whey, and suck the goat,
And cabin in a cave, and bring you up   180
To be a warrior and command a camp.   [*Exit with the Child.*

SCENE 12
*Outside the Emperor's
Palace.*
         SCENE III.   *Rome.   A public place.*
In the palace wall there
Enter TITUS, *bearing arrows with letters on the ends of them ; with him*   is a gateway. Y. LUCIUS
MARCUS, YOUNG LUCIUS, *and other gentlemen*, PUBLIUS, SEMPRONIUS,   checks that there are no
and CAIUS, *with bows.*   guards about and
                                                                  signals to TITUS that all
TIT. Come, Marcus, come ; kinsmen, this is the way.   is safe. TITUS gives Y.
Sir boy, let me see your archery ;   LUCIUS his bow and
Look ye draw home enough, and 'tis there straight.   takes his place at the
Terras Astrea reliquit,   head of his men, facing
Be you rememb'red, Marcus ; she's gone, she's fled.   5   the palace walls.
                                                                  Line 4: Latin spoken in
                                                                  English as 'The
                                                                  goddess of justice has
                                                              69 left the earth'.

Sirs, take you to your tools.   You, cousins, shall
Go sound the ocean and cast your nets ;
Happily you may catch her in the sea ;
Yet there's as little justice as at land.
No ; Publius and Sempronius, you must do it ;   10
'Tis you must dig with mattock and with spade,
And pierce the inmost centre of the earth ;
Then, when you come to Pluto's region,
I pray you deliver him this petition.
Tell him it is for justice and for aid,   15
And that it comes from old Andronicus,
Shaken with sorrows in ungrateful Rome.
Ah, Rome ! Well, well, I made thee miserable
What time I threw the people's suffrages
On him that thus doth tyrannize o'er me.   20
Go get you gone ; and pray be careful all,
And leave you not a man-of-war unsearch'd.
This wicked Emperor may have shipp'd her hence ;
And, kinsmen, then we may go pipe for justice.
MARC. O Publius, is not this a heavy case,   25
  To see thy noble uncle thus distract ?
PUB. Therefore, my lords, it highly us concerns
  By day and night t'attend him carefully,
  And feed his humour kindly as we may
  Till time beget some careful remedy.   30
MARC. Kinsmen, his sorrows are past remedy.
  Join with the Goths, and with revengeful war
  Take wreak on Rome for this ingratitude,
  And vengeance on the traitor Saturnine.
TIT. Publius, how now ? How now, my masters ?   35
  What, have you met with her ?
PUB. No, my good lord ; but Pluto sends you word,
  If you will have Revenge from hell, you shall.
  Marry, for Justice, she is so employ'd,
  He thinks, with Jove in heaven, or somewhere else,   40
  So that perforce you must needs stay a time.
TIT. He doth me wrong to feed me with delays.
  I'll dive into the burning lake below
  And pull her out of Acheron by the heels.
  Marcus, we are but shrubs, no cedars we,   45
  No big-bon'd men fram'd of the Cyclops' size ;
  But metal, Marcus, steel to the very back,
  Yet wrung with wrongs more than our backs can bear ;
  And, sith there's no justice in earth nor hell,
  We will solicit heaven, and move the gods   50
  To send down Justice for to wreak our wrongs.
  Come, to this gear.   You are a good archer, Marcus.   [He gives
                                              them the arrows.
  ' Ad Jovem ' that's for you ; here ' Ad Apollinem '.
  ' Ad Martem ' that's for myself.
  Here, boy, ' To Pallas ' ; here ' To Mercury '.   55
  ' To Saturn ', Caius—not to Saturnine :
  You were as good to shoot against the wind.
  To it, boy.   Marcus, loose when I bid.

The men draw their
bows. TITUS holds up
his hand, but instead of
giving the signal he
suddenly turns and
addresses them.

TITUS gives PUBLIUS a
petition. SATURNINUS
has refused to receive
any communications
from TITUS.
For 'What' read 'That'.
For 'thus' read 'now'.

Led by MARCUS they
leave TITUS alone,
staring at the palace
walls.

For 'Kinsmen' read
'My son', to clarify the
relationship of MARCUS
and PUBLIUS.

TITUS pulls a sheaf of
papers from his pocket.
Each is addressed to a
god. He hands them
out to the men who tie
the papers around the
arrows.

YOUNG LUCIUS looks
to MARCUS for
confirmation of the
order. To shoot arrows
into the Emperor's
Palace is dangerous.
The additional
70 messages make the
action even more risky.

Of my word, I have written to effect;
There's not a god left unsolicited.   60
MARC. Kinsmen, shoot all your shafts into the court;
We will afflict the Emperor in his pride.
TIT. Now, masters, draw. [*They shoot.*] O, well said, Lucius!   For 'said' read 'done'.
Good boy, in Virgo's lap!   Give it Pallas.   Lines 64–75 omitted.
MARC. My lord, I aim a mile beyond the moon;   65
Your letter is with Jupiter by this.
TIT. Ha! ha!
Publius, Publius, what hast thou done?
See, see, thou hast shot off one of Taurus' horns.
MARC. This was the sport, my lord: when Publius shot,   70
The Bull, being gall'd, gave Aries such a knock
That down fell both the Ram's horns in the court;
And who should find them but the Empress' villain?
She laugh'd, and told the Moor he should not choose
But give them to his master for a present.   75
TIT. Why, there it goes!   God give his lordship joy!

    Enter the CLOWN, *with a basket and two pigeons in it.*

News, news from heaven!   Marcus, the post is come.
Sirrah, what tidings?   Have you any letters?
Shall I have justice?   What says Jupiter?   79
CLO. Ho, the gibbet-maker?   He says that he hath taken them down   'Ho, the gibbet-maker'
again, for the man must not be hang'd till the next week.   spoken to camera.
TIT. But what says Jupiter, I ask thee?
CLO. Alas, sir, I know not Jupiter; I never drank with him in all my
life.   85
TIT. Why, villain, art not thou the carrier?
CLO. Ay, of my pigeons, sir; nothing else.
TIT. Why, didst thou not come from heaven?
CLO. From heaven!   Alas, sir, I never came there.   God forbid I
should be so bold to press to heaven in my young days.   Why, I
am going with my pigeons to the Tribunal Plebs, to take up a
matter of brawl betwixt my uncle and one of the Emperal's men.
MARC. Why, sir, that is as fit as can be to serve for your oration;
and let him deliver the pigeons to the Emperor from you.
TIT. Tell me, can you deliver an oration to the Emperor with a grace?   Line spoken by
CLO. Nay, truly, sir, I could never say grace in all my life.   MARCUS.
TIT. Sirrah, come hither.   Make no more ado,   100
But give your pigeons to the Emperor;
By me thou shalt have justice at his hands.
Hold, hold!   Meanwhile here's money for thy charges.
Give me pen and ink.   Sirrah, can you with a grace deliver up a   'Give me pen and ink'
supplication?   105   omitted.
CLO. Ay, sir.
TIT. Then here is a supplication for you.   And when you come to
him, at the first approach you must kneel; then kiss his foot;
then deliver up your pigeons; and then look for your reward.
I'll be at hand, sir; see you do it bravely.   111
CLO. I warrant you, sir; let me alone.
TIT. Sirrah, hast thou a knife?   Come let me see it.
Here, Marcus, fold it in the oration;
For thou hast made it like a humble suppliant.   115

Titus (Trevor Peacock) supervises the shooting of the letters to the gods

Tamora (Eileen Atkins) and Saturninus (Brian Protheroe)

And when thou hast given it to the Emperor,
Knock at my door, and tell me what he says.
CLO. God be with you, sir ; I will.
TIT. Come, Marcus, let us go.   Publius, follow me.   [*Exeunt.*   The CLOWN turns back
                                                                           to watch them leave.

SCENE IV.   *Rome.   Before the palace.*

Enter the EMPEROR, *and the* EMPRESS *and her two sons,* DEMETRIUS
and CHIRON ; LORDS *and* OTHERS.   *The* EMPEROR *brings the arrows*
in his hand that TITUS *shot at him.*

SAT. Why, lords, what wrongs are these !   Was ever seen
An emperor in Rome thus overborne,
Troubled, confronted thus ; and, for the extent
Of egal justice, us'd in such contempt ?
My lords, you know, as know the mightful gods,   5
However these disturbers of our peace
Buzz in the people's ears, there nought hath pass'd
But even with law against the wilful sons
Of old Andronicus.   And what an if
His sorrows have so overwhelm'd his wits,   10
Shall we be thus afflicted in his wreaks,
His fits, his frenzy, and his bitterness ?
And now he writes to heaven for his redress.
See, here's ' To Jove ' and this ' To Mercury ';
This ' To Apollo '; this ' To the God of War '-   15
Sweet scrolls to fly about the streets of Rome !
What's this but libelling against the Senate,
And blazoning our unjustice every where ?
A goodly humour, is it not, my lords ?
As who would say in Rome no justice were.   20
But if I live, his feigned ecstasies
Shall be no shelter to these outrages ;
But he and his shall know that justice lives
In Saturninus' health ; whom, if she sleep,
He'll so awake as he in fury shall   25
Cut off the proud'st conspirator that lives.

TAM. My gracious lord, my lovely Saturnine,
Lord of my life, commander of my thoughts,
Calm thee, and bear the faults of Titus' age,
Th' effects of sorrow for his valiant sons   30
Whose loss hath pierc'd him deep and scarr'd his heart ;
And rather comfort his distressed plight
Than prosecute the meanest or the best
For these contempts. [*Aside.*]   Why, thus it shall become
High-witted Tamora to gloze with all.   35
But, Titus, I have touch'd thee to the quick,
Thy life-blood out ; if Aaron now be wise,
Then is all safe, the anchor in the port.

Enter CLOWN.

How now, good fellow !   Wouldst thou speak with us ?

SCENE 13
The Senate.
SATURNINUS enters and
sits on a throne,
showing the arrows
with their messages
unrolled to the Senate.

The Senate rise in
anger at his accusation.
Appalled at his
behaviour they stand
watching as he tries to
break the arrows, fails,
and throws them on the
floor in a tantrum.

Lines 34–38 spoken to
camera.

The Senate settle down
again, calmed by
TAMORA's words.

CLO. Yes, forsooth, an your mistriship be Emperial.   40
TAM. Empress I am, but yonder sits the Emperor.
CLO. 'Tis he.—God and Saint Stephen give you godden. I have
    brought you a letter and a couple of pigeons here. [SATURNINUS
                                      reads the letter.

SATURNINUS discovers the knife in the letter and moves quickly towards his soldiers.

SAT. Go take him away, and hang him presently.   45
CLO. How much money must I have ?
TAM. Come, sirrah, you must be hang'd.
CLO. Hang'd ! by'r lady, then I have brought up a neck to a fair end.
                                      [Exit guarded.
SAT. Despiteful and intolerable wrongs !   50
    Shall I endure this monstrous villainy ?
    I know from whence this same device proceeds.
    May this be borne—as if his traitorous sons
    That died by law for murder of our brother
    Have by my means been butchered wrongfully ?   55
    Go drag the villain hither by the hair ;
    Nor age nor honour shall shape privilege.
    For this proud mock I'll be thy slaughterman,
    Sly frantic wretch, that holp'st to make me great,
    In hope thyself should govern Rome and me.   60

Enter NUNTIUS ÆMILIUS.

    What news with thee, Æmilius ?
ÆMIL. Arm, my lords ! Rome never had more cause.
    The Goths have gathered head ; and with a power
    Of high resolved men, bent to the spoil,
    They hither march amain, under conduct   65
    Of Lucius, son to old Andronicus ;
    Who threats in course of this revenge to do
    As much as ever Coriolanus did.

The Senate rise in consternation at the news of an attack, and look to SATURNINUS for guidance.

SAT. Is warlike Lucius general of the Goths ?
    These tidings nip me, and I hang the head   70
    As flowers with frost, or grass beat down with storms.
    Ay, now begins our sorrows to approach.
    'Tis he the common people love so much ;
    Myself hath often heard them say—
    When I have walked like a private man—   75
    That Lucius' banishment was wrongfully,
    And they have wish'd that Lucius were their emperor.
TAM. Why should you fear ? Is not your city strong ?
SAT. Ay, but the citizens favour Lucius,
    And will revolt from me to succour him.   80
TAM. King, be thy thoughts imperious like thy name !
    Is tne sun dimm'd, that gnats do fly in it ?
    The eagle suffers little birds to sing,
    And is not careful what they mean thereby,
    Knowing that with the shadow of his wings   85
    He can at pleasure stint their melody ;
    Even so mayest thou the giddy men of Rome.
    Then cheer thy spirit ; for know thou, Emperor,
    I will enchant the old Andronicus
    With words more sweet, and yet more dangerous,   90
    Than baits to fish or honey-stalks to sheep,

Lines 87–99 spoken as an aside.

Wh.n as the one is wounded with the bait,	Lines 92–99 spoken as
The other rotted with delicious feed.	an aside.

SAT. But he will not entreat his son for us.
TAM. If Tamora entreat him, then he will;   95
    For I can smooth and fill his aged ears
    Witn golden promises, that, were his heart
    Almost impregnable, his old ears deaf.
    Yet should both ear and heart obey my tongue.
    [*To* ÆMILIUS.] Go thou before to be our ambassador;   100
    Say that the Emperor requests a parley
    Of warlike Lucius, and appoint the meeting
    Even at his father's house, the old Andronicus.
SAT. Æmilius, do this message honourably;
    And if he stand on hostage for his safety,   105
    Bid him demand what pledge will please him best.
ÆMIL. Your bidding shall I do effectually.   [*Exit.*
TAM. Now will I to that old Andronicus,

And temper him with all the art I have,	Lines 108–110 spoken
To pluck proud Lucius from the warlike Goths. 110	to camera.

    And now, sweet Emperor, be blithe again,
    And bury all thy fear in my devices.
SAT. Then go successantly, and plead to him.   [*Exeunt.*

ACT FIVE

SCENE I. *Plains near Rome.*

Enter LUCIUS *with an army of* GOTHS *with drums
and colours.*

SCENE 14
*The Woods near Rome.
The Goth Camp.
There is a tree.*
LUCIUS marches in with
Roman soldiers. The
Goth princes give him
leave to address the
assembled company.

LUC. Approved warriors and my faithful friends,
    I have received letters from great Rome
    Which signifies what hate they bear their Emperor
    And how desirous of our sight they are.
    Therefore, great lords, be, as your titles witness,   5
    Imperious and impatient of your wrongs;
    And wherein Rome hath done you any scath,
    Let him make treble satisfaction.
1 GOTH. Brave slip, sprung from the great Andronicus,
    Whose name was once our terror, now our comfort,   10
    Whose high exploits and honourable deeds
    Ingrateful Rome requites with foul contempt,
    Be bold in us : we'll follow where thou lead'st,
    Like stinging bees in hottest summer's day,
    Led by their master to the flow'red fields,   15
    And be aveng'd on cursed Tamora.
ALL THE GOTHS. And as he saith, so say we all with him.
LUC. I humbly thank him, and I thank you all.
    But who comes here, led by a lusty Goth?

Spoken by 2 GOTH. All
the Goths then say:
'Aye'.

Enter a GOTH, *leading* AARON *with his* CHILD *in his arms.*

2 GOTH. Renowned Lucius, from our troops I stray'd   20

To gaze upon a ruinous monastery;
And as I earnestly did fix mine eye
Upon the wasted building, suddenly
I heard a child cry underneath a wall.
I made unto the noise, when soon I heard   25
The crying babe controll'd with this discourse:
'Peace, tawny slave, half me and half thy dam!
Did not thy hue bewray whose brat thou art,
Had nature lent thee but thy mother's look,
Villain, thou mightst have been an emperor;   30
But where the bull and cow are both milk-white,
They never do beget a coal-black calf.
Peace, villain, peace!'—even thus he rates the babe—   35
'For I must bear thee to a trusty Goth,
Who, when he knows thou art the Empress' babe,
Will hold thee dearly for thy mother's sake'.
With this, my weapon drawn, I rush'd upon him,
Surpris'd him suddenly, and brought him hither
To use as you think needful of the man.

LUC. O worthy Goth, this is the incarnate devil   40
That robb'd Andronicus of his good hand;
This is the pearl that pleas'd your Empress' eye;
And here's the base fruit of her burning lust.
Say, wall-ey'd slave, whither wouldst thou convey
This growing image of thy fiend-like face?   45
Why dost not speak? What, deaf? Not a word?
A halter, soldiers! Hang him on this tree,   Roman soldiers move
And by his side his fruit of bastardy.   with a rope to the tree,
AAR. Touch not the boy, he is of royal blood.   which has two ladders
LUC. Too like the sire for ever being good.   50 leaning against it.
First hang the child, that he may see it sprawl—
A sight to vex the father's soul withal.
Get me a ladder.   [*A ladder brought, which* AARON *is made to   AARON does not give up
                                              climb.*   the baby or climb the
AAR.   Lucius, save the child,   ladder at this point.
And bear it from me to the Emperess.
If thou do this, I'll show thee wondrous things   55
That highly may advantage thee to hear;
If thou wilt not, befall what may befall,
I'll speak no more but 'Vengeance rot you all!'
LUC. Say on; an if it please me which thou speak'st,
Thy child shall live, and I will see it nourish'd.   60
AAR. An if it please thee! Why, assure thee, Lucius,
'Twill vex thy soul to hear what I shall speak;
For I must talk of murders, rapes, and massacres,
Acts of black night, abominable deeds,
Complots of mischief, treason, villainies,   65
Ruthful to hear, yet piteously perform'd;
And this shall all be buried in my death,
Unless thou swear to me my child shall live.
LUC. Tell on thy mind; I say thy child shall live.
AAR. Swear that he shall, and then I will begin.   70
LUC. Who should I swear by? Thou believest no god;
That granted, how canst thou believe an oath?

AAR. What if I do not ?—as indeed I do not ;
Yet, for I know thou art religious
And hast a thing within thee called conscience,   75
With twenty popish tricks and ceremonies
Which I have seen thee careful to observe,
Therefore I urge thy oath.   For that I know
An idiot holds his bauble for a god,
And keeps the oath which by that god he swears,   80
To that I'll urge him.   Therefore thou shalt vow
By that same god—what god soe'er it be
That thou adorest and hast in reverence—
To save my boy, to nourish and bring him up ;
Or else I will discover nought to thee.   85
LUC. Even by my god I swear to thee I will.
AAR. First know thou, I begot him on the Empress.
LUC. O most insatiate and luxurious woman !
AAR. Tut, Lucius, this was but a deed of charity
To that which thou shalt hear of me anon.   90
'Twas her two sons that murdered Bassianus ;
They cut thy sister's tongue, and ravish'd her,
And cut her hands, and trimm'd her as thou sawest.
LUC. O detestable villain !   Call'st thou that trimming ?
AAR. Why, she was wash'd, and cut, and trimm'd, and 'twas   95
Trim sport for them which had the doing of it.
LUC. O barbarous beastly villains like thyself !
AAR. Indeed, I was their tutor to instruct them.
That codding spirit had they from their mother,
As sure a card as ever won the set ;   100
That bloody mind, I think, they learn'd of me,
As true a dog as ever fought at head.
Well, let my deeds be witness of my worth.
I train'd thy brethren to that guileful hole
Where the dead corpse of Bassianus lay ;   105
I wrote the letter that thy father found,
And hid the gold within that letter mention'd,
Confederate with the queen and her two sons ;
And what not done, that thou hast cause to rue,
Wherein I had no stroke of mischief in it ?   110
I play'd the cheater for thy father's hand,
And, when I had it, drew myself apart
And almost broke my heart with extreme laughter.
I pried me through the crevice of a wall,
When, for his hand, he had his two sons' heads ;   115
Beheld his tears, and laugh'd so heartily
That both mine eyes were rainy like to his ;
And when I told the Empress of this sport,
She swooned almost at my pleasing tale,
And for my tidings gave me twenty kisses.   120
GOTH. What, canst thou say all this and never blush ?
AAR. Ay, like a black dog, as the saying is.
LUC. Art thou not sorry for these heinous deeds ?
AAR. Ay, that I had not done a thousand more.
Even now I curse the day—and yet, I think,   125
Few come within the compass of my curse—

Right margin notes:

Lines 76–77 omitted.

Between lines 86 and 87: LUCIUS raises his hands and makes a formal oath to save the child. AARON gives him the baby and is then forced up the ladder and a noose placed around his neck. LUCIUS lays the baby on a shield at the foot of the tree.

Wherein I did not some notorious ill :
As kill a man, or else devise his death ;
Ravish a maid, or plot the way to do it ;
Accuse some innocent, and forswear myself ;   130
Set deadly enmity between two friends ;
Make poor men's cattle break their necks ;
Set fire on barns and hay-stacks in the night,
And bid the owners quench them with their tears.
Oft have I digg'd up dead men from their graves,   135
And set them upright at their dear friends' door
Even when their sorrows almost was forgot,
And on their skins, as on the bark of trees,
Have with my knife carved in Roman letters
' Let not your sorrow die, though I am dead '.   140
Tut, I have done a thousand dreadful things
As willingly as one would kill a fly ;
And nothing grieves me heartily indeed
But that I cannot do ten thousand more.
LUC. Bring down the devil, for he must not die   145
So sweet a death as hanging presently.
AAR. If there be devils, would I were a devil,
To live and burn in everlasting fire,
So I might have your company in hell
But to torment you with my bitter tongue !   150
LUC. Sirs, stop his mouth, and let him speak no more.

AARON, released from
the noose, attacks
LUCIUS but is
restrained by Roman
soldiers. LUCIUS then
thrusts a rag into
AARON's mouth.

Enter ÆMILIUS.

GOTH. My lord, there is a messenger from Rome   155
Desires to be admitted to your presence.
LUC. Let him come near.
Welcome, Æmilius.   What's the news from Rome ?
ÆMIL. Lord Lucius, and you Princes of the Goths,
The Roman Emperor greets you all by me ;
And, for he understands you are in arms,
He craves a parley at your father's house,
Willing you to demand your hostages,   160
And they shall be immediately deliver'd.
I GOTH. What says our general ?
LUC. Æmilius, let the Emperor give his pledges
Unto my father and my uncle Marcus.
And we will come.   March away.

[Exeunt.   As they march away
AARON looks back at the
baby.

SCENE II. *Rome.   Before Titus' house.*

*Enter TAMORA, and her two sons, DEMETRIUS
and CHIRON, disguised.*

TAM. Thus, in this strange and sad habiliment,
I will encounter with Andronicus,
And say I am Revenge, sent from below
To join with him and right his heinous wrongs.
Knock at his study, where they say he keeps   5
To ruminate strange plots of dire revenge ;

SCENE 15
*The back entrance to
Titus' House.*
Sides of meat are being
smoked. TAMORA and
her sons wear strange
make-up on their faces.
TAMORA's face looks
like a skull.
Lines 1–4 spoken to
camera.

Tell him Revenge is come to join with him,
And work confusion on his enemies.

They knock, and TITUS *opens his study door, above.*

TIT. Who doth molest my contemplation ?
Is it your trick to make me ope the door,   10
That so my sad decrees may fly away
And all my study be to no effect ?
You are deceiv'd ; for what I mean to do
See here in bloody lines I have set down ;
And what is written shall be executed.   15
TAM. Titus, I am come to talk with thee.
TIT. No, not a word.   How can I grace my talk,
Wanting a hand to give it that accord ?
Thou hast the odds of me ; therefore no more.
TAM. If thou didst know me, thou wouldst talk with me.   20
TIT. I am not mad, I know thee well enough :
Witness this wretched stump, witness these crimson lines ;
Witness these trenches made by grief and care ;
Witness the tiring day and heavy night ;
Witness all sorrow that I know thee well   25
For our proud Empress, mighty Tamora.
Is not thy coming for my other hand ?
TAM. Know thou, sad man, I am not Tamora :
She is thy enemy and I thy friend.
I am Revenge, sent from th' infernal kingdom   30
To ease the gnawing vulture of thy mind
By working wreakful vengeance on thy foes.
Come down and welcome me to this world's light ;
Confer with me of murder and of death ;
There's not a hollow cave or lurking-place,   35
No vast obscurity or misty vale,
Where bloody murder or detested rape
Can couch for fear but I will find them out ;
And in their ears tell them my dreadful name—
Revenge, which makes the foul offender quake.   40
TIT. Art thou Revenge ? and art thou sent to me
To be a torment to mine enemies ?
TAM. I am ; therefore come down and welcome me.
TIT. Do me some service ere I come to thee.
Lo, by thy side where Rape and Murder stands ;   45
Now give some surance that thou art Revenge—
Stab them, or tear them on thy chariot wheels ;
And then I'll come and be thy waggoner
And whirl along with thee about the globes.
Provide thee two proper palfreys, black as jet,   50
To hale thy vengeful waggon swift away,
And find out murderers in their guilty caves ;
And when thy car is loaden with their heads,
I will dismount, and by thy waggon wheel
Trot, like a servile footman, all day long,   55
Even from Hyperion's rising in the east
Until his very downfall in the sea.
And day by day I'll do this heavy task,

So thou destroy Rapine and Murder there.
TAM. These are my ministers, and come with me.   60
TIT. Are they thy ministers ?   What are they call'd ?
TAM. Rape and Murder ; therefore called so
    'Cause they take vengeance of such kind of men.
TIT. Good Lord, how like the Empress' sons they are !
    And you the Empress !   But we worldly men   65
    Have miserable, mad, mistaking eyes.
    O sweet Revenge, now do I come to thee ;
    And, if one arm's embracement will content thee,
    I will embrace thee in it by and by.   TITUS goes back
TAM. This closing with him fits his lunacy.   70   upstairs into his house.
    Whate'er I forge to feed his brain-sick humours,
    Do you uphold and maintain in your speeches,
    For now he firmly takes me for Revenge ;
    And, being credulous in this mad thought,
    I'll make him send for Lucius his son,   75
    And whilst I at a banquet hold him sure,
    I'll find some cunning practice out of hand
    To scatter and disperse the giddy Goths,
    Or, at the least, make them his enemies.
    See, here he comes, and I must ply my theme.   80

Enter TITUS, *below.*   TITUS comes out into
                                     the yard. TAMORA and
TIT. Long have I been forlorn, and all for thee.   the boys kneel as if for
    Welcome, dread Fury, to my woeful house.   some strange
    Rapine and Murder, you are welcome too.   ceremony. TITUS joins
    How like the Empress and her sons you are !   them.
    Well are you fitted, had you but a Moor.   85
    Could not all hell afford you such a devil ?
    For well I wot the Empress never wags
    But in her company there is a Moor ;
    And, would you represent our queen aright,
    It were convenient you had such a devil.   90
    But welcome as you are.   What shall we do ?
TAM. What wouldst thou have us do, Andronicus ?
DEM. Show me a murderer, I'll deal with him.
CHI. Show me a villain that hath done a rape,
    And I am sent to be reveng'd on him.   95
TAM. Show me a thousand that hath done thee wrong,
    And I will be revenged on them all.
TIT. Look round about the wicked streets of Rome,
    And when thou find'st a man that's like thyself,
    Good Murder, stab him ; he's a murderer.   100
    Go thou with him, and when it is thy hap
    To find another that is like to thee,
    Good Rapine, stab him ; he is a ravisher.
    Go thou with them ; and in the Emperor's court
    There is a queen, attended by a Moor ;   105
    Well shalt thou know her by thine own proportion,
    For up and down she doth resemble thee.
    I pray thee, do on them some violent death ;
    They have been violent to me and mine.
TAM. Well hast thou lesson'd us ; this shall we do.   110

But would it please thee, good Andronicus,
To send for Lucius, thy thrice-valiant son,
Who leads towards Rome a band of warlike Goths,
And bid him come and banquet at thy house ;
When he is here, even at thy solemn feast,   115
I will bring in the Empress and her sons,
The Emperor himself, and all thy foes ;
And at thy mercy shall they stoop and kneel,
And on them shalt thou ease thy angry heart.
What says Andronicus to this device ?   120
TIT. Marcus, my brother ! 'Tis sad Titus calls.

As MARCUS is heard
approaching TAMORA
and her sons bend low
to conceal their faces.

Enter MARCUS.

Go, gentle Marcus, to thy nephew Lucius ;
Thou shalt inquire him out among the Goths.
Bid him repair to me, and bring with him
Some of the chiefest princes of the Goths ;   125
Bid him encamp his soldiers where they are.
Tell him the Emperor and the Empress too
Feast at my house, and he shall feast with them.
This do thou for my love ; and so let him,
As he regards his aged father's life.   130
MARC. This will I do, and soon return again.   [*Exit.*
TAM. Now will I hence about thy business,
And take my ministers along with me.
TIT. Nay, nay, let Rape and Murder stay with me,
Or else I'll call my brother back again,   135
And cleave to no revenge but Lucius.
TAM. [*Aside to her sons.*] What say you, boys ? Will you abide with
    him,
Whiles I go tell my lord the Emperor
How I have govern'd our determin'd jest ?
Yield to his humour, smooth and speak him fair,   140
And tarry with him till I turn again.

| TIT. [*Aside.*] I knew them all, though they suppos'd me mad,

| Lines 142–144 spoken
| to camera.

| And will o'er-reach them in their own devices,
| A pair of cursed hell-hounds and their dam.
DEM. Madam, depart at pleasure ; leave us here.   145
TAM. Farewell, Andronicus, Revenge now goes
To lay a complot to betray thy foes.
TIT. I know thou dost ; and, sweet Revenge, farewell. [*Exit* TAMORA.
CHI. Tell us, old man, how shall we be employ'd ?

TITUS kisses TAMORA.
She leaves uncertainly.

TIT. Tut, I have work enough for you to do.   150
Publius, come hither, Caius, and Valentine.

Enter PUBLIUS, CAIUS, *and* VALENTINE.

PUB. What is your will ?
TIT. Know you these two ?
PUB. The Empress' sons, I take them : Chiron, Demetrius.
TIT. Fie, Publius, fie ! thou art too much deceiv'd.
The one is Murder, and Rape is the other's name ;
And therefore bind them, gentle Publius—
Caius and Valentine, lay hands on them.
Oft have you heard me wish for such an hour,   160

PUBLIUS, CAIUS,
VALENTINE and
SEMPRONIUS surround
CHIRON and
DEMETRIUS.

And now I find it ; therefore bind them sure,
And stop their mouths if they begin to cry.   [*Exit. They lay
                              hold on Chiron and Demetrius*
CHI. Villains, forbear ! we are the Empress' sons.
PUB. And therefore do we what we are commanded.
    Stop close their mouths, let them not speak a word.   165
    Is he sure bound ?   Look that you bind them fast.

CHIRON and DEMETRIUS try to break out of the encircling men. They are overpowered and tied up. YOUNG LUCIUS helps to gag them.

Re-enter TITUS ANDRONICUS *with a knife, and*
LAVINIA *with a basin.*

TIT. Come, come, Lavinia ; look, thy foes are bound.
    Sirs, stop their mouths, let them not speak to me ;
    But let them hear what fearful words I utter.
    O villains, Chiron and Demetrius !   170
    Here stands the spring whom you have stain'd with mud ;
    This goodly summer with your winter mix'd.
    You kill'd her husband ; and for that vile fault
    Two of her brothers were condemn'd to death,
    My hand cut off and made a merry jest ;   175
    Both her sweet hands, her tongue, and that more dear
    Than hands or tongue, her spotless chastity,
    Inhuman traitors, you constrain'd and forc'd.
    What would you say, if I should let you speak ?
    Villains, for shame you could not beg for grace.   180
    Hark, wretches ! how I mean to martyr you.
    This one hand yet is left to cut your throats,
    Whiles that Lavinia 'tween her stumps doth hold
    The basin that receives your guilty blood.
    You know your mother means to feast with me,   185
    And calls herself Revenge, and thinks me mad.
    Hark, villains ! I will grind your bones to dust,
    And with your blood and it I'll make a paste ;
    And of the paste a coffin I will rear,
    And make two pasties of your shameful heads ;   190
    And bid that strumpet, your unhallowed dam,
    Like to the earth, swallow her own increase.
    This is the feast that I have bid her to,
    And this the banquet she shall surfeit on ;
    For worse than Philomel you us'd my daughter,   195
    And worse than Progne I will be reveng'd.
    And now prepare your throats.   Lavinia, come,
    Receive the blood ; and when that they are dead,
    Let me go grind their bones to powder small,
    And with this hateful liquor temper it ;   200
    And in that paste let their vile heads be bak'd.
    Come, come, be every one officious
    To make this banquet, which I wish may prove
    More stern and bloody than the Centaurs' feast.   [*He cuts their
                                                        throats.*
    So.
    Now bring them in, for I will play the cook,   205
    And see them ready against their mother comes.   [*Exeunt,
                                                bearing the dead bodies.*

Lines 198–201, 'and when that . . . be bak'd', omitted.

As TITUS leaves, Y. LUCIUS stares at the bodies, and at LAVINIA who is holding up a bowl with her stumps to catch the blood.

212

SCENE III. *The court of Titus' house.*

Enter LUCIUS, MARCUS, *and the* GOTHS, *with* AARON *prisoner, and his*
CHILD *in the arms of an* ATTENDANT.

LUC. Uncle Marcus, since 'tis my father's mind
    That I repair to Rome, I am content.
I GOTH. And ours with thine, befall what fortune will.
LUC. Good uncle, take you in this barbarous Moor,
    This ravenous tiger, this accursed devil ;   5
    Let him receive no sust'nance, fetter him,
    Till he be brought unto the Empress' face
    For testimony of her foul proceedings.
    And see the ambush of our friends be strong ;
    I fear the Emperor means no good to us.   10
AAR. Some devil whisper curses in my ear,
    And prompt me that my tongue may utter forth
    The venomous malice of my swelling heart !
LUC. Away, inhuman dog, unhallowed slave !
    Sirs, help our uncle to convey him in.   [*Exeunt* GOTHS *with*
                                AARON. *Flourish within.*
    The trumpets show the Emperor is at hand.

Sound trumpets. *Enter* SATURNINUS *and* TAMORA, *with* ÆMILIUS,
    TRIBUNES, SENATORS, *and* OTHERS.

SAT. What, hath the firmament more suns than one ?
LUC. What boots it thee to call thyself a sun ?
MARC. Rome's Emperor, and nephew, break the parle ;
    These quarrels must be quietly debated.   20
    The feast is ready which the careful Titus
    Hath ordain'd to an honourable end,
    For peace, for love, for league, and good to Rome.
    Please you, therefore, draw nigh and take your places.
SAT. Marcus, we will.   [*A table brought in.* *The company sit down.*

Trumpets sounding, enter TITUS *like a cook, placing the dishes, and*
    LAVINIA *with a veil over her face ; also* YOUNG LUCIUS, *and* OTHERS.

TIT. Welcome, my lord ; welcome, dread Queen ;
    Welcome, ye warlike Goths ; welcome, Lucius ;
    And welcome all.   Although the cheer be poor,
    'Twill fill your stomachs ; please you eat of it.
SAT. Why art thou thus attir'd, Andronicus ?   30
TIT. Because I would be sure to have all well
    To entertain your Highness and your Empress.
TAM. We are beholding to you, good Andronicus.
TIT. An if your Highness knew my heart, you were.
    My lord the Emperor, resolve me this :   35
    Was it well done of rash Virginius
    To slay his daughter with his own right hand,
    Because she was enforc'd, stain'd, and deflower'd ?
SAT. It was, Andronicus.

                                            213

SCENE 16
*A Public Place in
Rome.*
AARON is led on as a
captive. Y. LUCIUS
presents LUCIUS with
water to wash his hands
before he approaches
the altar to light the
ceremonial flame. The
Goths who accompany
LUCIUS are uncertain of
the ritual.

AARON suddenly breaks
from the soldiers and
sweeps all the
ceremonial objects
from the altar. He
throws water and puts
out the ceremonial
flame.

SATURNINUS holds out
his hand to LUCIUS who
refuses to kiss it.

Led by YOUNG LUCIUS,
the whole company
process into Titus'
house.

SCENE 17
Titus' House.
A banquet is laid.
TITUS and LAVINIA
stand with the servants
to receive their guests.
TITUS cuts the pie.
Y. LUCIUS gives LAVINIA
his dagger, then he and
TITUS take a plate each,
one for SATURNINUS
and one for TAMORA.
LAVINIA, TITUS and Y.
LUCIUS sit watching in
silence as they eat.
LAVINIA raises her veil.
TITUS rises and
approaches
SATURNINUS.

TIT. Your reason, mighty lord.   40
SAT. Because the girl should not survive her shame,
  And by her presence still renew his sorrows.
TIT. A reason mighty, strong, and effectual ;
  A pattern, precedent, and lively warrant
  For me, most wretched, to perform the like.   45
  Die, die, Lavinia, and thy shame with thee ;   [*He kills her.*
  And with thy shame thy father's sorrow die !
SAT. What hast thou done, unnatural and unkind ?
TIT. Kill'd her for whom my tears have made me blind.
  I am as woeful as Virginius was,   50
  And have a thousand times more cause than he
  To do this outrage ; and it now is done.
SAT. What, was she ravish'd ? Tell who did the deed.
TIT. Will't please you eat ? Will't please your Highness feed ? | TITUS throws the pie on
TAM. Why hast thou slain thine only daughter thus ?   55 | the table.
TIT. Not I ; 'twas Chiron and Demetrius.
  They ravish'd her, and cut away her tongue ;
  And they, 'twas they, that did her all this wrong.
SAT. Go, fetch them hither to us presently.
TIT. Why, there they are, both baked in this pie,   60
  Whereof their mother daintily hath fed,
  Eating the flesh that she herself hath bred.
  'Tis true, 'tis true : witness my knife's sharp point.   [*He stabs
                                   the Empress.* | SATURNINUS overturns
SAT. Die, frantic wretch, for this accursed deed !   [*He stabs Titus.* | the table in order to
LUC. Can the son's eye behold his father bleed ? | reach TITUS.
  There's meed for meed, death for a deadly deed.   [*He stabs* | Y. LUCIUS tries to
Saturninus. A great tumult. LUCIUS, MARCUS, *and their* FRIENDS | prevent his father from
go up into the balcony. | killing SATURNINUS.

MARC. You sad-fac'd men, people and sons of Rome,
  By uproars sever'd, as a flight of fowl
  Scatter'd by winds and high tempestuous gusts, | SCENE 18
  O, let me teach you how to knit again   70 | *A Public Place in*
  This scattered corn into one mutual sheaf, | *Rome.*
  These broken limbs again into one body ; | PUBLIUS enters
  Lest Rome herself be bane unto herself, | carrying a box as
  And she whom mighty kingdoms curtsy to, | MARCUS speaks to the
  Like a forlorn and desperate castaway,   75 | Tribunes and Senate
  Do shameful execution on herself. | from a high platform.
  But if my frosty signs and chaps of age, | Y. LUCIUS sits by the
  Grave witnesses of true experience, | body of TITUS. The
  Cannot induce you to attend my words, | bodies of LAVINIA,
  [*To* LUCIUS.] Speak, Rome's dear friend, as erst our ancestor, | TAMORA and
  When with his solemn tongue he did discourse   81 | SATURNINUS are also
  To love-sick Dido's sad attending ear | laid out.
  The story of that baleful burning night, | LUCIUS, in formal
  When subtle Greeks surpris'd King Priam's Troy. | bonds because he has
  Tell us what Sinon hath bewitch'd our ears,   85 | killed the Emperor,
  Or who hath brought the fatal engine in | kneels to AEMILIUS who
  That gives our Troy, our Rome, the civil wound. | releases him.
  My heart is not compact of flint nor steel ;
  Nor can I utter all our bitter grief,
  But floods of tears will drown my oratory   90

Young Lucius (Paul Davies-Prowles) tries to restrain his father Lucius (Gavin Richards) from killing Saturninus (Brian Protheroe)

Marcus (Edward Hardwicke) proclaims Lucius emperor

And break my utt'rance, even in the time
When it should move ye to attend me most,
And force you to commiseration.
Here's Rome's young Captain, let him tell the tale ;
While I stand by and weep to hear him speak. 95

LUC. Then, gracious auditory, be it known to you
That Chiron and the damn'd Demetrius
Were they that murd'red our Emperor's brother ;
And they it were that ravished our sister.
For their fell faults our brothers were beheaded, 100
Our father's tears despis'd, and basely cozen'd
Of that true hand that fought Rome's quarrel out
And sent her enemies unto the grave.
Lastly, myself unkindly banished,
The gates shut on me, and turn'd weeping out, 105
To beg relief among Rome's enemies ;
Who drown'd their enmity in my true tears,
And op'd their arms to embrace me as a friend.
I am the turned forth, be it known to you,
That have preserv'd her welfare in my blood 110
And from her bosom took the enemy's point,
Sheathing the steel in my advent'rous body.
Alas ! you know I am no vaunter, I ;
My scars can witness, dumb although they are,
That my report is just and full of truth. 115
But, soft ! methinks I do digress too much,
Citing my worthless praise. O, pardon me !
For when no friends are by, men praise themselves.

MARC. Now is my turn to speak. Behold the child. [*Pointing to*
the Child in an Attendant's arms.
Of this was Tamora delivered, 120
The issue of an irreligious Moor,
Chief architect and plotter of these woes.
The villain is alive in Titus' house,
Damn'd as he is, to witness this is true.
Now judge what cause had Titus to revenge 125
These wrongs unspeakable, past patience,
Or more than any living man could bear.
Now have you heard the truth : what say you, Romans ?
Have we done aught amiss, show us wherein,
And, from the place where you behold us pleading, 130
The poor remainder of Andronici
Will hand in hand all headlong hurl ourselves,
And on the ragged stones beat forth our souls,
And make a mutual closure of our house.
Speak, Romans, speak ; and if you say we shall, 135
Lo, hand in hand, Lucius and I will fall.

ÆMIL. Come, come, thou reverend man of Rome,
And bring our Emperor gently in thy hand,
Lucius our Emperor ; for well I know
The common voice do cry it shall be so. 140

ALL. Lucius, all hail, Rome's royal Emperor !

MARC. Go, go into old Titus' sorrowful house,
And hither hale that misbelieving Moor

LUCIUS speaks from the raised platform.
PUBLIUS hands MARCUS the box.

LUCIUS shows his scars.

MARCUS opens and holds up the box, which contains the body of AARON's child.

As LUCIUS goes towards the throne, Y. LUCIUS listens to the whispered conversation of MARCUS and PUBLIUS as he stares at the box.

86

To be adjudg'd some direful slaught'ring death,
As punishment for his most wicked life.   *[Exeunt some*
    ATTENDANTS. LUCIUS, MARCUS, *and the* OTHERS *descend.*

ALL. Lucius, all hail, Rome's gracious governor !

LUC. Thanks, gentle Romans ! May I govern so
To heal Rome's harms and wipe away her woe !
But, gentle people, give me aim awhile,
For nature puts me to a heavy task.   150
Stand all aloof ; but, uncle, draw you near
To shed obsequious tears upon this trunk.
O, take this warm kiss on thy pale cold lips.   *[Kisses Titus.*
These sorrowful drops upon thy blood-stain'd face,
The last true duties of thy noble son !   155

MARC. Tear for tear and loving kiss for kiss
Thy brother Marcus tenders on thy lips.
O, were the sum of these that I should pay
Countless and infinite, yet would I pay them !

LUC. Come hither, boy ; come, come, and learn of us   160
To melt in showers. Thy grandsire lov'd thee well ;
Many a time he danc'd thee on his knee,
Sung thee asleep, his loving breast thy pillow ;
Many a story hath he told to thee,
And bid thee bear his pretty tales in mind   165
And talk of them when he was dead and gone.

MARC. How many thousand times hath these poor lips,
When they were living, warm'd themselves on thine !
O, now, sweet boy, give them their latest kiss !
Bid him farewell ; commit him to the grave ;   170
Do them that kindness, and take leave of them.

BOY. O grandsire, grandsire ! ev'n with all my heart
Would I were dead, so you did live again !
O Lord, I cannot speak to him for weeping ;
My tears will choke me, if I ope my mouth.   175

      Re-enter ATTENDANTS *with* AARON.

A ROMAN. You sad Andronici, have done with woes ;
Give sentence on the execrable wretch
That hath been breeder of these dire events.

LUC. Set him breast-deep in earth, and famish him ;
There let him stand and rave and cry for food.   180
If any one relieves or pities him,
For the offence he dies. This is our doom.
Some stay to see him fast'ned in the earth.

AAR. Ah, why should wrath be mute and fury dumb ?
I am no baby, I, that with base prayers   185
I should repent the evils I have done ;
Ten thousand worse than ever yet I did
Would I perform, if I might have my will.
If one good deed in all my life I did,
I do repent it from my very soul.   190

LUC. Some loving friends convey the Emperor hence,
And give him burial in his father's grave.
My father and Lavinia shall forthwith

[Right margin:]
LUCIUS ascends the
throne and places the
laurel crown on his
head. The assembled
company kneel.

AARON is brought out of
Titus' house. He sees
the box and knows
what is inside.
Spoken by AEMILIUS.

Be closed in our household's monument.
As for that ravenous tiger, Tamora,   195
No funeral rite, nor man in mourning weed,
No mournful bell shall ring her burial ;
But throw her forth to beasts and birds to prey.
Her life was beastly and devoid of pity,
And being dead, let birds on her take pity.

[*Exeunt.*   MARCUS looks at YOUNG
            LUCIUS, who has
            opened the box and is
            staring at the baby's
            body within. Slowly
            MARCUS closes the box.
            YOUNG LUCIUS stares
            into space.

GLOSSARY

Geoffrey Miles

Difficult phrases are listed under the most important or most difficult word in them. If no such word stands out, they are listed under the first word.

Words appear in the form they take in the text. If they occur in several forms, they are listed under the root form (singular for nouns, infinitive for verbs).

Line references are given only when the same word is used with different meanings, and when there are puns.

Line numbers of prose passages are counted from the last numbered line before the line referred to (since the numbers given do not always correspond to those in this edition).

A-BED, 'is brought a-bed', has given birth
ABIDE, stay
ABOUT, to go about, V ii 132
ABOVE, see ALOFT, V ii 8 *stage direction*
ABUSED, wronged, deceived
ACCITED, summoned
ACCORD, 'to give it that accord', to provide the appropriate gestures to make it graceful
ACCOUNT OF, consider, value
ACHERON, a river in the Underworld (perhaps used as a general name for Hell)
ACHIEVE, 'what you cannot ... as you may', what you cannot achieve in the way you want, you must achieve however you can
ACTAEON, in Greek mythology, a hunter who accidentally came upon Diana (*see* DIAN) bathing; the angry goddess turned him into a deer, and he was torn to pieces by his own hounds
AD, (Latin) to; 'Ad Jovem ... Apollinem ... Martem', To Jove (or Jupiter) ... Apollo ... Mars; 'Ad manes fratrum', to the spirits of (our) brothers
ADJUDG'D, sentenced to
ADMITS, consents to, acknowledges as legitimate
ADVANCE, promote, raise in status
ADVANCED, raised
ADVANTAGE (v.), be of benefit to
ADVENT'ROUS, adventurous, brave
ADVICE, 'upon advice', after thinking about it; 'by good advice', by a carefully considered plan

ADVISE, 'advise thee', consider
AENEAS, (alluding to Virgil's *Aeneid*, Book II, where Aeneas tells Dido the story of the fall of Troy, beginning 'You ask me to renew an unspeakable grief'; *see also* DIDO)
AETNA, Mount Etna, a volcano in Sicily
AFFECT, desire
AFFECTED, loved
AFFORD, be capable of providing, III i 44; provide with, V ii 86
AFFY, have faith
AFOOT, 'well afoot', up and about
AFTER, afterwards, II iii 3, 123; 'after me', as I have done
AGAINST, 'against their mother comes', for the coming of their mother
AGE, 'mine age', i.e. the fact that I am the elder, I i 8; 'faults of Titus' age', misdeeds Titus commits as a result of his old age
AGREE, 'full well agree', are entirely consistent
AIM, see GIVE ... AIM, V iii 149
AJAX, a Greek hero of the Trojan War. He had a contest with Ulysses ('Laertes' son') for the arms of Achilles, was defeated, went mad with rage and killed himself; Ulysses persuaded the other Greeks to give him a hero's funeral
ALCIDES, a name for Hercules, the Greek hero of supernatural strength and courage
ALEHOUSE PAINTED SIGNS, (notoriously crude and garish)
ALOFT, on a raised place on the Elizabethan stage (perhaps a gallery at the back of the stage), I i 1 *stage direction*

ALOOF, aside

AMAIN, at full speed

AMBUSH, 'ambush of our friends', i.e. a Gothic force lying in wait in case of treachery by Saturninus

AMISS, 'Have we done aught amiss', If we have done anything wrong

AN, if; 'an if', if

ANCESTOR, 'our ancestor', i.e. Aeneas

ANCHORAGE, anchors

AND, 'and at this day ... of the Goths' (these lines, which are inconsistent with the rest of the scene, are probably part of a cancelled first draft); 'obtain and ask', obtain if you ask; 'And what not done ... in it?', i.e. What was done ... that I did not have a hand in? (The syntax is confused); 'And ours with thine', And our intention ('mind') is the same as yours; 'and basely cozen'd', and our father was basely cheated

ANNOY (n.), trouble

ANSWER, answer for, I i 412; 'answer their suspicion', see SUSPICION

APOLLO, Roman god of the sun, patron of healing and oracles

APPARENT, obvious, clear

APPOINT, arrange

APPOINTED, equipped

APPROVE, prove

APPROVED, of proven quality

ARIES, the constellation of the Ram, in the zodiac

ARIGHT, correctly

AS, (often) like; that, IV iv 25; such as, V i 128; 'as good as Saturninus may', even a man as exalted as Saturninus may (be cuckolded); 'as who should say', as if he were saying, IV ii 121; 'as who ... justice were', as if to say there is no justice in Rome

ASPIR'D, risen

ASSURE, 'assure thee', you may be sure

AT HEAD, (a metaphor from bull-baiting, where the bravest dog would go for the nose)

ATTEND, stay beside, IV i 28, 126; listen to, V iii 79, 93

ATTENDING, listening

AUDITORY, listeners

AUGHT, anything

AUTHOR, 'author to dishonour you', the cause of your being dishonoured

AVAUNT, get away! be gone!

AY ME, alas! (a cry of grief)

BADGE, see VULCAN'S BADGE, II i 89

BANDY, (i) brawl, (ii) form a gang

BANE, destroyer

BANQUET, a light meal of sweetmeats, fruit and wine, III ii 1 *stage direction*

BARK, ship, I i 71

BAUBLE, the stick carried by a court fool

BAY, deep, prolonged barking of hounds, II ii 3; 'at such a bay', cornered like that (a hunting metaphor)

BE, let ... be, III i 243

BEAR, 'bear his name', i.e. be called 'life' (when it is really death)

BEAR-WHELPS, bear-cubs (i.e. Chiron and Demetrius)

BECOME, 'shall become', must be the proper course of action for

BECOMES, is fitting (for)

BEFALL, 'befall what may befall', 'befall what fortune will', whatever happens

BEFRIEND, do a favour to

BEGUILE, distract attention from

BEHOLDING, indebted

BEING, 'being dead', now she is dead

BELIEVEST, believe in

BELIKE, probably

BELONGS, 'here is more belongs to her', she ought to have more done to her

BENT, 'bent to the spoil', intent on plunder

BERAY'D, disfigured, defiled

BEREFT, deprived

BESTOW, provide, IV ii 164

BETIDE, happen to

BEWET, made wet

BEWRAY, reveal, II iv 3; betray, V i 28

BEYOND, 'beyond their feeling', *see* FEELING

BID, tell ... to; bade, told to, II iii 186, IV ii 13; invited, I i 338, V ii 193

BIDE, remain

BIND, confine, III i 221

BIRDS, young ones, II iii 154

BLABB'D, uttered (without the modern derogatory sense)

BLACKAMOOR, black

BLAZONING, publicly proclaiming

BLISS, (i.e. heaven)

BLITHE, cheerful

BLOWSE, (usually) a ruddy-faced, plump girl (here used ironically of a black boy)

BOAST, proud display

BODES, portends

BOLD, confident, V i 13

BONDMEN, slaves

BONJOUR, 'good day', a morning greeting

BOON, favour

BOOTLESS, useless, III i 75; uselessly, III i 36

BOOTS, 'What boots it thee', What good does it do you (since the comparison is obviously absurd)

BOOTY, see HOPEFUL, II iii 49

BOUND, indebted, IV ii 172; see LAUREL, I i 74

BOWELS, interior, III i 97; inside of (my)body (punning on the 'bowels' of the earth), III i 231

BRABBLE, squabble

BRAIN-SICK, crazy

BRAT, child (not necessarily a term of abuse)

BRAVE (v.), defy, IV ii 36, 137; 'brave it', swagger boldly

BRAVELY, very well

BRAVES (n.), (i) boasts, (ii) challenges, II i 30

BRAVING, (i) boasting, swaggering, (ii) challenging (one another)

BRAWL, see TAKE UP, IV iii 90–1

BREAK, 'break the parle', break up the exchange (of insults); 'break up utt'rance', interrupt my speech

BREATH'D, uttered

BREEDER, origin, V iii 178

BREEDERS, women, mothers, IV ii 68

BRINE-PIT, pit of salt water

BRING, 'bring . . . asleep', send to sleep

BRINISH, briny, salty

BROACH, stick on a spit

BROACH'D, begun

BROOK, endure

BROUGHT A-BED, see A-BED

BRUTUS, see JUNIUS BRUTUS

BURNING LAKE, (probably the fiery river Phlegethon in the Underworld)

BUT, (often) only; (often) except; 'but that . . . we can', that we cannot; 'but I will find', without me finding; 'had you but', if only you had

BUZZ, spread rumours

BY, 'by this', by this time; 'By me', as a result of my influence

BY AND BY, soon

BY'R LADY, by Our Lady (a mild oath)

CABIN, live, make your home

CAESAR, title of the Roman Emperor

CAME, 'I never came there', I have never been there

CANDIDATUS, (Latin) a candidate (literally, one dressed in white, as Roman candidates for office were)

CANST THOU TELL, you want to bet?

CAPITOL, the temple of Jupiter Optimus Maximus on the Capitoline Hill, the central temple of Rome

CAPTAIN, general, V 3 94

CAR, chariot

CAREFUL, requiring trouble to bring about, IV iii 30; (i) taking trouble, (ii) afflicted with cares, V iii 22; 'is not careful', does not worry

CASE, state of affairs

CASTAWAY, reprobate, sinner in a state of despair

CASTLE, 'writing . . . enemy castle', i.e. spattering the enemy stronghold with blood

CAUCASUS, see PROMETHEUS

CAUSE, case, dispute, I i 59; 'cause of Rome', mission on behalf of Rome; 'an 'twere my cause', if I were in her position

'CAUSE, because

CAUSELESS, without good reason

CEDARS, (traditionally the tallest type of tree)

CENTAURS' FEAST, a battle between the Centaurs (half-horse, half-men) and the Lapiths (a Greek tribe) which took place at the wedding feast of the Lapith king Pirithous. It is described in bloody detail in Ovid's *Metamorphoses*, Book XII

CERBERUS, the fierce three-headed dog who guarded the entrance to the Underworld. He was once lulled to sleep by the lyre of Orpheus ('the Thracian poet'), who came to rescue his wife Eurydice from death

CHAFED, enraged

CHALLENGED, accused

CHANCE, (bad) luck

CHANCED, which happened

CHANGING, fickle

CHAPS, cracks in the skin

CHARGES, (i.e. the pigeons), IV iii 103

CHARMING, spellbinding (much stronger than the modern sense)

CHASE, hunting-ground

CHEATER, (i) escheator, an official appointed to look after property forfeited to the state, (ii) cheat, swindler (pun)

CHEER, facial expression, I i 264; entertainment (i.e. food), V iii 28

CHOICE, 'damn'd her loathed choice', may the loathsome man she chose (Aaron) be damned

CHOOSE, 'he should not choose but', he ought not to do anything else but

CHURL, a rude, ill-bred person (usually male)

CIMMERIAN, one of a legendary race who lived in perpetual darkness (hence, a black person)

CIRCUMSCRIBED, encircled, confined within limits

CIRCUMSTANCE, 'the circumstance of all', all the details

CITING, 'citing my worthless praise', talking about the praise I do not deserve

CIVIL, inflicted in civil war

CLEAN, entirely

CLEAVE, 'cleave to ... Lucius', stick to Lucius as my only hope for revenge

CLIME, climate (believed to cause skin colour)

CLOSE, secret, IV ii 118; tightly, V ii 165

CLOSED, enclosed

CLOSET, room

CLOSING, 'This closing ... lunacy', This pretence of agreeing with him (about 'Rapine and Murder') is the appropriate way of dealing with his lunacy

CLOSURE, see MUTUAL, V iii 134

CLOUDY, darkened by grief, I i 263; gloomy, sullen, II iii 33

CLOWN, (i) rustic, (ii) comedian

CLOY'D, glutted, satiated

CLUBS, CLUBS! (the cry raised in London's streets for help to break up a riot)

COCYTUS, one of the rivers of the Underworld (used here to mean Hell, whose entrance was often shown in the medieval miracle plays as a mouth emitting smoke and flames)

CODDING, (perhaps) lustful (from 'cod', testicle)

COFFIN, (i) pie-crust, (punning on) (ii) funeral casket

COIL, fuss

COIN, produce (with a pun on the literal sense)

COMING, 'Is not thy coming for', Have you not come for

COMMON, 'common voice', voice of the common people

COMMONWEAL, commonwealth, state

COMPACT, composed

COMPASS, range

COMPASSION (v.), have pity on

COMPLOT, (i) plot, conspiracy, (ii) plot outline (punning on the theatrical sense of 'plot', an outline of the action of a play hung up backstage as a guide to the actors), II iii 265

CONCEIT, clever device

CONDUCT, leadership

CONDUCTED, led

CONDUIT, water-pipe (an image borrowed from Ovid's description of the death of Pyramus in *Metamorphoses*, Book IV)

CONFIDENT, trustful

CONFLICT, i.e. love-making (an ironic euphemism)

CONFOUND, destroy

CONFUSION, ruin, destruction; 'work confusion on', destroy

CONSECRATE, consecrated, made sacred

CONSTRAIN'D, raped

CONTINENCE, self-restraint (not necessarily sexual)

CONTROL, restrain, III i 260; 'controll'd with', restrained by, V i 26; 'controll'd', opposed, thwarted, I i 420

CONTROLLER, censorious critic

CONTROLMENT, being restrained

CONVENIENT, 'It were convenient you had', It would be appropriate for you to have

CORDIAL, comfort (literally, a medicine that stimulates the heart)

CORIOLANUS, Gaius Marcius Coriolanus, a Roman general of the early Republic (around 400 BC) who, after being banished by the people, joined with the enemy state of the Volscians and led a foreign army to sack Rome; he was turned back at the last moment by the pleas of his mother. (He is the hero of Shakespeare's later tragedy *Coriolanus* (about 1608))

CORNELIA, the mother of the Gracchi (Tiberius and Gaius Gracchus, Roman tribunes and political reformers of the 1st century BC), who was famous for her devotion to her sons

COUCH, lie hidden

COUNSEL, 'keep counsel', keep a secret; 'Two may ... away' (proverbial)

COUNSEL-KEEPING, which kept their secret

COUNSELS, plans

COURSE, plan of action, IV i 120

COURT, 'court it', play the suitor

COUSIN, (here) niece (used loosely for any relative outside one's immediate family), II iv 12

COZEN'D, cheated

CRAVES, asks for

CREATE, create emperor

CROSS, 'be cross', pick a quarrel

CRY, 'cry of hounds', deep barking in unison

CULL'D, picked

CURTSY TO, do honour to

CUT OFF, put to death

CYCLOPS, a mythical race of one-eyed giants

DAM, mother (of an animal), i.e. Tamora, II iii 142, IV i 98; 'the devil's dam', the devil's mother (proverbially worse than the devil himself)

DAME, lady

DANCING-RAPIER, sword worn only as an ornament, like a dancer's

DATE, duration

DAYS, 'no longer days', no more time

DAZZLE, (of eyes) become blurred from strain

DEAD, 'at dead time of the night', at dead of night (with ominous overtones)

DEADLY-STANDING, fixed in a stare like a dead man's (or which causes death)

DEAR, (punning on 'deer'), III i 91; expensive (with a pun on the sense 'loved'), III i 200; dire, grievous, III i 257

DECEIV'D, wrong

DECIPHER'D ... FOR, detected as

DECREED, decided

DECREES, decisions, resolutions

DEEP, profound, intense (of feelings)

DEEPER, 'thou art ... better skill'd' (i.e. than to read children's schoolbooks)

DEFENDER, 'Thou great defender', i.e. Jupiter (see CAPITOL)

DEGENERATE, (i.e. so lacking in spirit that he will let his wife be stolen)

DELIVERED, 'is delivered', has given birth (but Aaron pretends to take it in the modern sense), IV ii 61

DENIES, forbids

DESERT, 'let desert ... shine', let the fact that I deserve the throne be made clear in your uncorrupted choice (of me); 'none of both ... desert', both of you have deserved great rewards

DESPITE, 'in my despite', in spite of me

DESPITEFUL, cruel, malicious

DETECT, expose

DETERMINE, decide; 'determin'd jest', see GOVERN'D

DEVICE, scheming, trickery, I i 395; plan, II i 79, IV iv 112; (i) plan, contrivance, (ii) plan for a theatrical performance (pun), III i 134; enigmatic design accompanied by a motto, e.g. on a shield (here, the knife wrapped in a letter), IV iv 52; 'in their own devices', through their own plots

DIADEM, crown

DIAN, or Diana, the virgin goddess of hunting, chastity, and the moon

DIDO, Queen of Carthage, who fell in love with the Trojan exile Aeneas ('the wand'ring prince'). Caught in a storm during a hunt, they took refuge in a cave and there consummated their love, with tragic consequences. The story is told in Virgil's *Aeneid*, Book IV

DIE, 'all quarrels die', let all quarrels die

DIREFUL, dreadful

DISCOURSE (n.), 'this discourse', these words; (v.) relate, V iii 81

DISCOVER, reveal

DISPATCH'D, carried out

DISPOSE, deposit

DISTIL, fall in drops

DISTRACT, mad

DIVINING, 'true divining', truly guessing

DOMINATOR, in astrology, the planet or sign of the zodiac under which a person was born, which determined his or her character

DONE, had sexual intercourse with (a common pun), IV ii 76

DOOM, sentence; 'my ... banishment', a sentence of banishment for life on me; 'doom her death', condemn her to death

DOTE, talk or act foolishly

DOUBTED, suspected

DREAD, inspiring awe

DREADFUL, inspiring dread

DREW, 'drew myself apart', stood aside

DRIVE, rush

DRUMS AND TRUMPETS, i.e. drummers and trumpeters

DUMB SHOWS, mimes (a theatrical term)

DUMPS, melancholy

DURST, dared

EARTH, 'Like to the earth ... increase' (because the dead are buried in their Mother Earth)

EASE, 'do thee ease', help or comfort thee

ECSTASIES, fits of madness

ECSTASY, madness

EDGE, 'wants edge', are dull

EFFECTED, carried out

EFFECTLESS, useless ('effectless use' is deliberately paradoxical)

EFFECTUAL, to the point

EFFECTUALLY, effectively, with the intended result

EGAL, equal, impartial

ELECT, choose

ELECTION, choice; 'in election', as a candidate

EMBRACEMENT, embrace

EMPERAL, (the Clown's blunder for 'Emperor')

EMPERESS, empress

EMPERIAL, imperial

EMPERY, imperial power, the position of emperor

EMPIRE, the position of emperor

EMPLOY'D, busy; 'how . . . employ'd, what are we to do?

ENACTS, resolutions

ENCELADUS, one of the Titans, giants who made war against the gods in Greek mythology

ENCOUNTER WITH, meet with; 'encounter'd with', met by

END, purpose, V iii 23; 'to a worthy end', (i) for a valuable purpose, (ii) to meet a noble ending

ENFORC'D, raped

ENFRANCHISED, set free

ENGINE, instrument (i.e. the tongue), III i 82; (i.e. the Wooden Horse), V iii 86

ENGINES, wits, minds

ENSIGNS, tokens, symbols

ENTRAILS, interior

ENTREATS, 'at entreats', to entreaties

ENVIOUS, malevolent

ENVIRON'D WITH, surrounded by

ENVY, hate, malice

ERST, once

ESCAPE, escapade

EVEN, (often a meaningless intensifier); 'even with', in exact agreement with, IV iv 8

EXCLAIMS, exclamations, outcries

EXECUTION, 'do . . . execution on', kill

EXPECTING, 'expecting . . . when', waiting for the time when

EXTENT, 'for the extent . . . justice', as a result of the exercise of equal (i.e. impartial) justice

EXTREMES, excesses (of emotion)

FACT, crime

FAGOT, stick of firewood

FAIR, courteously, I i 46; handsome, II i 92; (i) fair-skinned, (ii) handsome, (iii) just, honest (a triple pun), III i 205; 'speak him fair', see SPEAK

FALL TO, begin eating

FAME, 'house of Fame', house of Rumour (described by Ovid as having a thousand doors, always open, and brass walls which echo and amplify every whisper)

FAT, 'doth fat me', is as good as a banquet to me

FATAL, ominous (the raven's cry was thought to be a bad omen), II iii 97, 202; 'fatal-plotted', contrived (or written down) to cause death

FATHERS, i.e. Senators (*patres*, 'fathers', was their Latin title), III i 1

FAULT, offence, crime

FEALTY, loyalty to a lord

FEAR, fear for

FEARFUL, 'fearful slumber', terrifying sleep (Titus imagines himself in a nightmare)

FEED, 'feed his humour(s)', indulge his whims

FEELING, 'beyond their feeling', though they do not feel it (because of their stupidity)

FELL, savage, cruel

FERE, husband (or wife)

FIE, (an exclamation of protest)

FILE, 'file our engines', sharpen our wits

FIND, 'find it', find it true; 'find . . . out', detect

FIRMAMENT, sky

FIT, make ready, II i 12; furnish with what you need, IV i 115

FITS (n.), bursts of passion; (v.) befits, I i 187; 'fits not with this hour', is not appropriate for this moment

FITTED, 'Well are you fitted', You would be well set up (to represent Tamora and co.)

FLATTERING, deluding

FLATT'RY, delusion, self-deception

FLOURISH, fanfare of trumpets

FLOURISH'D, 'flourish'd . . . with his sword', brandished his sword

FLOUTED AT, mocked

FOLD, conceal (in the wrinkles of a smile)

FOND, foolish

FOOL, poor thing (a term of endearment or pity), III ii 20; 'What fool . . . sea' (proverbial)

FOOT, 'the better foot before', step lively!

FOR, (often) because; for the sake of, I i 259; fit for, III ii 58; in return for, V i 115; out of, V ii 180; 'for virtue's praise', to be praised for your virtue; 'for his life', to save his life; 'for fear', in fear; 'for thee', out of longing for you (Revenge), V ii 81

FOR THAT, because

FOR TO, to

FOR WHY, because

FORBEAR, stop

FORC'D, raped, IV i 52, V ii 178

FORFEND, forbid

FORGE, invent

FORLORN, lost, II iii 153; forsaken, desperate, V ii 81, V iii 75

FORSOOTH, indeed

FORSWEAR, perjure

FORTH, out (of)

FORTHWITH, immediately

FORTUNE, (good) luck; (Whose wisdom . . . conquered', who has overcome her misfortune by strength of mind (or cunning)

FORWARD, 'forward in my right', keen in support of my cause

FOWL, birds

FRANTIC, mad

94

FRANTICLY, crazily
FRAUGHT, freight
FRENZY, madness
FROM, 'From the place ... pleading' (presumably Marcus and Lucius are now on a raised part of the stage; see ALOFT)
FROSTY, 'frosty ... chaps', white hair and cracks in the skin
FRUIT, offspring
FULL, (often) very; fully, II i 57
FUMBLE, wrap up clumsily
FURY, 'Whose fury ... griefs', (i.e. the fact that he cannot conceal his rage shows that his grief is genuine); 'but in fury', except in a fit of madness; 'Fury', one of a group of spirits, in Greek mythology, who pursued and punished evildoers, V ii 82

GAD, spike
GALLANT, see GROOMS, IV ii 165
GALL'D, irritated
GALLOPS, gallops through
GEAR, 'to this gear', let's get on with this business
GENERAL, 'our general name' (i.e. the name of woman)
GENTLE, (often) noble
GENTLENESS, nobility, noble generosity
GET YOU GONE, go, be on your way
GIBBET-MAKER, maker of gallows (the Clown's misunderstanding of 'Jupiter')
GIDDY, fickle, unreliable
GILT, gilded
GIVE ... AIM, encourage, support (?)
GLAD, gladden
GLISTERING, glistening
GLOBES, the earth and the other planets (?)
GLOZE, use smooth talk
GO TO; Come off it! (an impatient exclamation)
GODDEN, 'God ... give you godden', God give you good even (a colloquial greeting)
GOOD, 'You were as good to shoot', you would do as much good by shooting
GOODLIEST, finest
GOODLY, beautiful, handsome, fine; excellent (ironical), IV iv 19
GOT, begotten
GOTHS, a Germanic barbarian people, who invaded the Roman Empire in the 3rd, 4th and 5th centuries AD
GOVERN, control, III i 219; 'govern'd our determin'd jest', carried out the joke we decided on
GOVERNOR, ruler

GRAC'D, favoured
GRACE (n.), favour, I i 480; II i 34; mercy, I i 455, II iii 182, V ii 180; God's favour which helps men to be good, III i 205; 'with a grace', gracefully (but the Clown takes the word in the sense of 'a blessing before a meal'); (v.), adorn, make graceful, V ii 17
GRACIOUS, (often a meaningless term of respect); acceptable, pleasing, I i 11, 170, 429, II i 32; favourable, I i 60, 78
GRACIOUSLY, kindly, generously, I i 381; with favour, I i 439
GRAMERCY, thanks
GRAMMAR, Lily's Latin grammar, a standard Elizabethan school text, in which these lines of Horace are quoted
GRANDSIRE, grandfather
GRATIFY, give pleasure to
GRATULATE, congratulate him on
GRAVE, having weight and dignity (translating the Latin gravis), III i 1; sober, respectable, III i 43; 'Grave witnesses of', which give weighty evidence of my
GREET, greet one another, I i 90
GREY, (often used to describe a cold, clear, early-morning sky)
GROOMS, 'gallant grooms', splendid fellows, IV ii 165
GROUND, basis, cause, II i 48; 'this discord's ground', (i) the cause of this quarrel, (ii) the bass line against which this discordant descant is raised (a musical pun)
GRUDGE, quarrel, enmity
GUILEFUL, treacherous

HABILIMENT, costume
HABITED, dressed
HADST, (i.e. obtained), II iii 145
HALE, draw, drag
HALTER, noose
HAND, 'lend me thy hand', help me, give me a hand (with the obvious pun)
HANDLE, 'handle not the theme', don't discuss the subject (with a pun on 'hand')
HANDSOMELY, conveniently
HANG, hover upon, III ii 61
HAP, 'it is thy hap', you happen
HAPPILY, perhaps
HAPPY, fortunate
HARK YE, listen
HARMS, injuries
HE, 'he comforts you', he who comforts you
HEAD, 'gathered head', raised an army
HEAP, 'all on a heap', in a fallen mass

HEART, mind, thoughts, feelings, II iv 34, V iii 34; 'with all my heart', very gladly

HEARTILY, profoundly, to the heart, V i 143

HEAVINESS, sorrow, III ii 49

HEAVY, sad, sorrowful

HECTOR, the greatest Trojan hero in the Trojan War ('the Roman Hector' is probably Lucius, though perhaps Titus)

HECUBA, wife of Priam, King of Troy. During the Trojan War she sent her youngest son Polydorus for safe keeping to Polymestor, King of Thrace ('the Thracian tyrant'), who murdered him for his treasure. After the fall of Troy Hecuba discovered this crime; in revenge she arranged a meeting with Polymestor and his sons at which she murdered his sons and blinded him; at last she went mad, and was changed into a dog

HENCE, away from here; 'let us hence', let us go away

HER, (i.e. Rome's), V iii 110

HERE, 'Here's no sound jest', see JEST

HIE, go quickly

HIGH, noble, great

HIGH-WITTED, cunning

HIM, (i.e. Saturninus), V i 8; (i.e. Lucius), V ii 76

HIS, its, III i 97; his relatives, IV iv 23; 'his first-born ... of Rome', the first-born son of the man who was the last Emperor of Rome; 'by honour of his name ... succeed', (perhaps) by the honour in which you hold the candidate you (each) support

HIT, 'hit it', (i) hit the nail on the head, (ii) 'scored' (Aaron picks up the sexual double meaning)

HITHER, here, to this place

HOLD, wait!, IV iii 103; 'hold thee dearly', consider you dear

HOLP'ST, helped

HOME, fully back, IV iii 3

HONESTY, chastity

HONEY-STALKS, stalks of clover (poisonous to sheep in large amounts)

HONOUR, 'doth make ... body's hue', makes your reputation as black as his body

HOPE, 'in hope', in the hope that; see STAND, II i 119

HOPEFUL, 'our hopeful booty', the victims we hope to catch

HOPES, hopes for, II iii 41

HORNING, 'gift in horning', talent for giving people horns (the old joke that a cuckolded husband grew horns on his forehead)

HOUSE, 'house of Fame', see FAME

HOW NOW, (an expression of greeting, often suggesting impatience or protest: 'What's going on?')

HUE, (i) appearance, (ii) complexion, I i 261

HUMOUR(S), whims, caprices, irrationalities

HYMENAEUS, the Roman god of marriage

HYPERION, the Sun (god)

IGNOMY, ignominy, disgrace

ILL (adv.), badly, wickedly, III i 235; (n.) evil, V i 127

ILL-FAVOUR'D, ugly

IMAGE, statue, III i 259

IMPATIENT (OF), unwilling to endure (opposition, etc)

IMPERIOUS, (i) imperial, (ii) majestic, commanding

IN, against, II iv 291; 'in my blood', by shedding my own blood; 'in part of', see PART

INCORPORATE, made a part (of)

INCREASE, offspring

INDIFFERENTLY, impartially

INGRATEFUL, ungrateful

INHERIT, possess

INSINUATE, curry favour

INSULT ON, exult or gloat over

INTEGER VITAE ... ARCU, (Latin) 'The man who is upright of life and free from crime does not need the javelins or bow of the Moor.' (A quotation from the *Odes* (I.22) of the Roman poet Horace (Quintus Horatius Flaccus). Presumably with a veiled allusion to Aaron the Moor)

INTEND, intend to perform, I i 78

INTERCEPT, interrupt

INTEREST, legal claim to or title in something; 'where life ... breathe', where one's only claim to be 'alive' is that one is still breathing

ISSUE, offspring

JAR, 'join for that you jar', combine to get what you are quarrelling over

JEST, 'Here's no sound jest', This isn't funny!

JET, encroach

JOVE, or Jupiter, king of the Roman gods

JOY (v.), enjoy, II iii 83

JUNIUS BRUTUS, a Roman nobleman who avenged the rape of Lucrece by leading the revolution which drove out the Tarquin kings; see also LUCRECE

JUST, exactly, IV ii 24

JUSTICE, 'justice ... health', justice exists so long as Saturninus is alive and well

KEEP, guard, I i 12; carry on making, IV ii 57; stay, IV ii 134

KEEPER'S, gamekeeper's

KEEPS, spends his time, V ii 4

KIND (adj.), having natural affection, I i 61; (n.) Nature, II i 116; natural disposition, II iii 281

KING, (often) Emperor

KNEW, 'knew she', even if she did know

KNIT, tie, knot

LACKS, 'lacks but', there is nothing missing but

LAERTES' SON, Ulysses or Odysseus (see AJAX)

LAMENTING DOINGS, lamentations (?)

LANGOUR, grief

LANGUISHMENT, pining for love, mooning around

'LARUMS, alarums, trumpet calls

LATEST, last

LATH, wooden sword (a common stage prop)

LAUREL, 'bound with laurel boughs', wearing a laurel wreath on his head (as a symbol of victory)

LAVE, wash

LAY, 'lay it by', put it away; 'lay hands on', seize

LEAGUE, alliance

LEARN, teach, II iii 143

LEAVE (n.), 'give me leave', let me speak; 'losers will have leave' (proverbial: i.e. the defeated, being harmless, can be allowed to speak freely); (v.) cease, III ii 46; 'leave to plead', stop pleading

LEER, complexion (with a pun on the modern sense?)

LEISURE, (I'll trust by leisure', I'll not be in a hurry to trust

LESSON'D, instructed

LET, 'let me alone', leave it to me; 'let alone', stop doing it

LIGHTLY, easily, casually

LIKE, dressed as, V iii 25 stage direction; 'like a private man', disguised as an ordinary citizen

LIMBO, a region outside Hell, occupied by the souls of unbaptised children and virtuous pagans, who could never enter Heaven ('bliss')

LION, (i.e. Saturninus; the lion was a symbol of royalty), IV i 99

LIQUOR, liquid

LIST, likes

LIVELY, living, III i 105; 'lively warrant', striking justification

LO, see, behold

LOADEN, loaded

LONG, for a long time

LOOK, expect, III i 202; be careful that, III ii 1; 'look for', expect

LOOSE (adj.), promiscuous; (v.) let go, II iii 245; release (an arrow), IV iii 58

LORD JUNIUS BRUTUS, see JUNIUS BRUTUS

LOVE-DAY, (i) a day appointed for settling disputes, (ii) a day for making love (pun)

LUCRECE, or Lucretia, wife of a Roman senator, was raped by young Tarquin, the son of King Tarquin the Proud. She told the story to her family, and then killed herself. Her husband and father, and their friend Lucius Junius Brutus, raised a revolution, drove the Tarquins out of Rome, and established the Roman Republic. (The story is told in Shakespeare's long poem *The Rape of Lucrece*)

LUSTY, vigorous

LUXURIOUS, lecherous

MADDED, driven mad

MADE AWAY, disposed of, killed; 'The midwife . . . made away' (i.e. once they have been disposed of)

MADE UNTO, made for

MAGNI DOMINATOR POLI . . .?, (Latin) 'Lord of the great heavens, are you so slow to hear and to see crimes?' (A slightly inaccurate quotation from the play *Phaedra* (or *Hippolytus*) by the Roman dramatist Seneca)

MAKE, 'make her sure', see SURE; 'how much she makes of thee', how much attention she is giving you

MAN-OF-WAR, warship

MAP, image, embodiment

MARK, pay attention to

MARK'D, destined, chosen (to die), I i 125; 'mark'd with', guilty of

MARKS, observes

MARRY, (a mild oath: 'by the Virgin Mary')

MARTYR (v.), mutilate; 'martyr'd signs', mutilated gestures (i.e. the broken gestures she makes in spite of her mutilations)

MASTER, i.e. the queen bee (thought in Shakespeare's time to be male), V i 15

MATTER, see TAKE UP, IV iii 90–1

MAUGRE, in spite of

MEAN, means, way of achieving an end, II iv 40

MEANER, lower (in rank)

MEANEST, 'the meanest or the best', those of lowest or highest rank

MEED, reward; 'meed for meed', measure for measure, i.e. a fitting recompense

MEET, suitable

MERCURY, the messenger of the Roman gods

MESH'D, mashed, brewed

METHINKS, it seems to me

MIGHTFUL, mighty

MILDLY, 'mildly as we might', as mild as we could do

MILLER, 'more water ... miller of' (proverbial: i.e. people can't see everything that goes on)

MIND, thoughts, II iv 3, V i 69; intention, V iii 1; 'her mind', what was in her mind

MINE, 'and therefore mine' (i.e. my hand shall go)

MINION, hussy

MINISTERS, agents

MISBELIEVING, falsely believing (usually meaning non-Christian)

MISCHIEF, harm, evildoing

MISCHIEFS, injuries

MISS, fail

MISTRISHIP, ladyship

MOCK, piece of mockery

MOCKS, imitates (i.e. echoes)

MONUMENT, tomb

MORE, (punning on 'Moor'), IV ii 53; 'that would she for twenty thousand more' (i.e. she would say amen to a prayer for twenty thousand Roman ladies to be raped)

MOTHER, 'for our ... mother's care' (i.e. for the sake of our mother's loving care for us)

MOTION, proposal

MOUNT, 'mount her pitch', rise to the highest point of her flight (a term from falconry)

MUTINY, riot

MUTUAL, whose parts belong together, V iii 71; 'mutual closure', common end

MYSELF, I, IV iv 74

NAPKIN, handkerchief

NEEDFUL OF, necessary for

NEEDS, necessarily

NE'ER A WHIT, not a bit

NICE-PRESERVED, carefully preserved

NILUS, the River Nile (famous for its yearly floods)

NIP, injure (of the effect of frost on plants)

NO MORE, say no more, V ii 19

NOR ... NOR, neither ... nor

NOT, 'Not far, one Muliteus', Not far away (there lives) one Muliteus (Aaron changes his construction in the middle of the sentence; but the text may be corrupt)

NOTED, notorious

NOTHING, 'Nothing ... pitful', not nearly as kind as the ravens, but still showing some pity

NOURISH, bring up, nurse

NUNTIUS, (Latin) messenger

NURS'D, 'They have nurs'd ... life', i.e. by feeding me they have kept me alive only to suffer this woe

OBJECT, (i) sight, spectacle, (ii) thing

OBSCURE, (i) dark, (ii) remote, hidden

OBSEQUIES, funeral rites

OBSEQUIOUS, dutiful towards the dead (without the modern derogatory sense)

ODDS, 'odds of', advantage over

O'ERFLOW, become flooded

O'ER-REACH, get the better of, V ii 143

OF, from, II i 2, IV iv 102; V i 90; for, IV ii 171; about, V ii 34; on, V ii 63; by, V iii 36; 'of my word', upon my word

OFFICIOUS, busy (without the modern derogatory sense)

OLYMPUS, Mount Olympus, on whose summit the gods were said to live; 'climbeth ... Olympus' top', has reached the summit of ambition

ONSET, beginning

OP'D, opened

OPE, open

OPINION, reputation

OPPOSE, compare

ORDAIN'D, organised

OUT, is out, IV iv 37

OUT ALAS! alas! ('out' is an exclamation of horror or grief)

OUT OF HAND, on the spur of the moment

OUT ON THEE, shame on you!

OUTLIVE, survive, II iii 132

OUTRAGEOUS, excessive, immoderate

OVERCOME, overgrown

OVERLOOKS, looks down upon

OVERSHINE, (i) shed light on, (ii) outshine

OVER-WEEN, show arrogant overconfidence

OVID'S METAMORPHOSES, a poem in fifteen books by the Roman poet Publius Ovidius Naso (43 BC–AD 17), retelling many of the Greek legends, linked by the theme of changes of shape, in a vivid, half-serious, half-humorous manner. Shakespeare almost certainly read it at school, and undoubtedly knew the translation by Arthur Golding (1593); it had a great influence on him, and *Titus Andronicus* is full of Ovidian allusions

PACK, conspire

PAINTED, artificial, imaginary, II iii 126

PALFREYS, riding-horses

PALLAS, or Athena, goddess of knowledge

PALLIAMENT, the white gown of a candidate for the Roman consulship

PANTHEON, a Roman temple dedicated to all the gods

PARCEL, part

PARLE, discussion

PART (n.), side, I i 446; 'in part of', as part payment for; (v.) depart, I i 488

PARTY, see SPECIAL, I i 20–1

PASS'D, given, I i 468; 'there nought hath pass'd But', nothing has happened except

PASSING, extremely

PASSION, grief, I i 106, III ii 48

PASSIONATE (v.), express passionately

PASSIONS, passionate outbursts, III i 218

PASTIES, pies

PATIENCE, control yourself, I i 203, III i 138; 'under your patience', if you don't mind my saying so (ironically polite); 'past patience', impossible to bear

PATIENT (v.), calm

PATRICIANS, the Roman noble class

PATRON, champion; 'patrons of my right', upholders of my claim to the throne

PATTERN, model, precedent

PATTERN'D BY, designed on the model of

PAWS, (i.e. claws), II iii 152

PEACE, be silent, (here) stop crying, III ii 50

PEAL, 'hunter's peal', blowing of hunting horns

PER STYGA, PER MANES VEHOR, (Latin) 'I am borne over the Styx and through the ranks of ghosts', i.e. I am in hell; see also STYX. (Adapted from a line in Seneca's play *Phaedra*)

PERCHANCE, perhaps

PERFECT, i.e. word-perfect

PERFORCE, necessarily

PHILOMEL, or Philomela, an Athenian princess whose sister Progne was the wife of Tereus, King of Thrace. Tereus conceived a lust for Philomel, trapped her in an isolated cottage in the woods and raped her, then cut out her tongue to stop her betraying the crime. Philomel revealed the story by weaving it into a tapestry which she sent to Progne. The sisters then took revenge on Tereus by killing his young son Itys and serving his flesh to Tereus at a banquet. The legend is told in Ovid's *Metamorphoses*, Book VI, and clearly lies behind the story of Lavinia

PHILOMELA, see PHILOMEL

PHOEBE, goddess of the moon (another name for Diana)

PHYSIC, medicine (ironical)

PIECE, woman (contemptuous and slangy)

PIETY, the Roman virtue of duty and reverent obedience towards the gods, one's country, and one's parents and family

PIPE FOR, whistle for, i.e. search in vain for

PITCH, see MOUNT, II i 14

PIUS, (Latin) dutiful, having the virtue of piety (see PIETY)

PLAIN, flat, IV i 70

PLANET, (alluding to the influence of the planets, in astrology, which by unfavourable positions could produce sudden misfortune, sickness or death), II iv 14

PLAY'D, 'play'd your prize', won your bout (a phrase from fencing)

PLEASE, 'Please you', 'would it please thee . . . To' (formally polite forms of request)

PLEASURE, 'at pleasure', whenever he likes

PLEBEIANS, the common people of Rome

PLEDGE, hostage; (Lucius' family are hostages for his good behaviour in exile), III i 292

PLIES, urges, keeps on at

PLUTO, the Roman god of the Underworld

PLY, 'ply my theme', carry on with my argument

POLICY, cunning, clever strategy (usually with the implication of cynical unscrupulousness)

PONIARD, dagger

POSSIBILITY, 'speak with possibility', speak of things that are possible

POST, messenger

POWER, POW'R, army

PRACTICE, scheme

PRESENT, immediate

PRESENTLY, immediately

PRETEND, claim (not necessarily falsely)

PREVAILING, successful

PREY, 'to prey', for them to prey on her

PRIAM, King of Troy, who had fifty sons, most of whom died in the Trojan War

PRIED ME, peered

PRINCES, leaders, V i 156, V ii 125

PRIVILEGE, see SHAPE, IV iv 57

PRIZE, see PLAY'D, I i 399

PRODIGIES, unnatural events, portents

PROGNE, see PHILOMEL

PROMETHEUS, a Titan who stole fire from heaven to give it to mankind, and was punished by the gods by being chained to a rock in the Caucasus (a mountain range in southern

Russia), where a vulture continually gnawed his body

PROMISE, assure, II iii 196

PROPER, handsome

PROPORTION, bodily form

PROPOSE, be willing to meet

PROSECUTE, carry out

PROVIDE, 'provide thee', provide yourself with

PURCHASE, 'purchase ... friends', obtain our lasting friendship

PUT, 'put up', sheathe (a sword); 'put it up', put up with it (the image is of 'sheathing' a quarrel; see the previous meaning); 'puts me to', requires me to perform

PYRAMUS, (Pyramus and Thisbe were young lovers who arranged to meet secretly by moonlight. Thisbe arrived first, but was scared off by a lion; Pyramus, finding her cloak torn on the ground, believed her dead, and killed himself, as did Thisbe when she returned to find him dead. The story is told in Ovid's *Metamorphoses*, Book IV; Shakespeare later turned it to farce in *A Midsummer Night's Dream*)

QUARREL, (often) cause (in a war)

QUEEN OF TROY, *see* HECUBA

QUIT, requite, pay back

QUOTES, examines

RAGGED, rough

RANSOM, fine paid to obtain pardon, III i 156

RAPINE, rape

RATED, berated, abused

RATES, scolds

REAR, raise

REASON, 'do myself ... right', obtain what is mine both in reason and in justice; 'great reason', it is no wonder

RECEIVED FOR, taken for

REDEEM, ransom, free by paying a price

RE-EDIFIED, rebuilt

REFLECT, shine

REGARDS, cares about

RELIGIOUSLY, (i) as a religious duty, (ii) strictly, conscientiously

REMAINETH, 'remaineth naught', there is nothing left to do

REMEMB'RED, 'be you rememb'red', remember

REMIT, pardon

RENT, rend, tear

REPAIR, return

REPREHENDING, reproaching

REPROACH, disgrace

REPUTE, consider

REQUIRE, ask

REQUITE, avenge, III i 297

RE-SALUTE, greet again

RESERV'D, saved up

RESOLVE, 'resolve me this', answer this question for me

REST, (i) remain, (ii) relax peacefully (pun), IV ii 31

REVENGE, 'Revenge the heavens', Let the heavens take revenge

REVEREND, to be revered

RIGHT, 'in the Capitol and Senate's right', in the name of the Capitol and the Senate; 'do me right', give me justice; 'in right ... of', in defence of the rightful cause of

ROSED, rosy

RUDE-GROWING, roughly growing

RUE, have pity on, I i 105; regret, V i 109

RUFFLE, swagger

RUIN, (i.e. mutilated body), III i 208

RUTHFUL, piteous

RUTHLESS, without pity

SAD, morose, grim, II iii 10; dismal-looking, V ii 1; solemn, V ii 11

SALUTES, greets

SAMPLER, piece of embroidery

SANGUINE, (i) ruddy-faced, (ii) dominated by the humour of the blood (in the medieval theory of the four humours, sanguine people were red-complexioned, brave, impulsive and extroverted. Aaron himself is melancholy, dominated by black bile: dark, secretive and reserved)

SATURN, a Roman god, father of Jupiter, IV iii 56; the planet Saturn, which, in astrology, caused bad luck and disaster and produced gloomy, sluggish, cold personalities, II iii 31

SATURNINE, (another form of Saturninus)

SCATH, harm

SCORN, object of contempt, I i 265

SCROWL, (i) gesticulate with the arms, (ii) scrawl, scribble, (iii) write as if on a scroll (a triple pun)

SCYTHIA, an ancient region (in modern Russia) whose inhabitants were known for cannibalism and other barbaric practices

SEAL, 'thy seal', *see* STAMP, IV ii 69

SEARCH, probe (a surgical term)

SECURELY, (i) free from care, (ii) over-confidently

SELF, 'of that self-blood', by the same blood

SEMIRAMIS, a legendary queen of Babylon, famous for beauty, pride, lust and cruelty
SENSIBLY, plainly, obviously (?)
SEQUENCE, 'in sequence', one after the other
SEQUEST'RED, separated
SERVE, be my mistress's 'servant' (a cliché of the language of courtly love), II i 36; satisfy, indulge, II i 130; 'serve your turns', 'serve the turn', see TURN
SET (n.), game, V i 100; (v.) 'set abroad', start off; 'set fire on', set fire to
SHADOWS, shades, ghosts, I i 100; illusions, unreal things, III ii 80
SHALL, 'shall be', am to be, III i 180; 'say we shall', tell us to do it, V iii 135
SHAME (v.), feel ashamed, III i 15
SHAPE, 'shape privilege', create immunity
SHIFT, stratagem, IV i 73; 'puts us to our shifts', forces us to adopt stratagems
SHIVE, slice; 'easy it is ... shive' (proverbial: i.e. a married woman is easily seduced)
SHOULD, 'should have', was to have
SHRINK, withdraw, slip away
SIBYL'S LEAVES, (the Sibyl of Cumae, a legendary prophetess, wrote her prophecies on leaves, which were often blown away before anyone could read them)
SIGHING, 'wound it was sighing' (alluding to the belief that each sigh drained a drop of blood from the heart)
SIGHT, 'of our sight', to see us
SINGLE, (a hunting term for separating one animal from the rest of the herd in order to hunt it down); 'are singled forth', have separated yourselves from the others
SINK, cesspool, sewer
SINON, the Greek spy whose lies persuaded the Trojans to bring the Wooden Horse into Troy
SIREN, in Greek mythology, a mermaid whose spellbinding song lured travellers to their death on the rocks
SIRRAH, fellow (a term of address to inferiors, sometimes expressing contempt, as at III ii 75)
SIT FAS AUT NEFAS, (Latin) 'be it right or wrong'
SITH, since
SLAUGHTERMAN, executioner
SLIP, cutting from a plant, (hence) offspring
SLIPS, moral lapses (i.e. Tamora's adulteries)
SMOKE, 'smoke for it', suffer for it
SMOOTH, flatter, humour
SMATCH, (i) swift catch, (ii) snack

SO, (often) so long as, on condition that (e.g. II i 102, III i 22); by doing that, II iii 179; as a result, V ii 11
SOFT, quiet!; Enough of this, V iii 116
SOLEMN, ceremonial, II i 112, V ii 115
SOLICIT, petition
SOLON, a Greek sage who declared that no man should be called 'happy' until he was dead (and therefore safe from ill fortune)
SOME, 'some deal', to some extent
SOMETIME, sometimes
SOMEWHAT, something
SOMEWHITHER, (to) somewhere
SORROW, lamentation, III i 119
SORROW-WREATHEN, folded in sorrow (folded arms were a conventional pose expressing grief or melancholy)
SORT, way III i 191; 'in some sort', in a way
SOUND, see JEST, IV ii 26
SPEAK, 'speak him fair', humour him
SPECIAL, 'for whom we stand A special party', as whose representatives we (the Tribunes) have a special constitutional role (?)
SPEED, be successful, II i 101; 'if all the rest will speed' (obscure: if everything in future is to go well? if the rest of you wish to live?)
SPLEENFUL, lustful (the spleen was thought to be the seat of the passions)
SPOIL, see BENT, IV iv 64
SPORT, entertainment; amusing thing, IV iii 70; 'their sports', turned into entertainment for them
SPOTLESS, unstained
SPOTTED, stained
SPOUSAL, marriage
SPRAWL, writhe in pain
SPURN, contemptuous kick
SQUARE, quarrel, II i 100; 'square yourselves', quarrel with one another (?); frame, shape, III ii 31
STALE, (i) laughing-stock, (ii) decoy, distraction (Saturninus implies that Titus has offered Lavinia to him merely as a cover for her affair with Bassianus)
STAMP, 'thy stamp, thy seal', something labelled as yours as clearly as if you had marked it with your seal (the personal design stamped in wax to seal a letter)
STANCH, satisfy
STAND, 'stand ... in hope', have a chance of success; 'stand on', insists on a
STAR, i.e. position of the stars (believed in astrology to control destinies), IV ii 32
STARVED, dying of cold

STAY, stop, wait; 'stay your strife', stop arguing; 'stay'd', kept

STILL (adj.), continual, III ii 45; (adv.) always, constantly, continually

STINT, put a stop to

STOMACHS, passion, anger, III i 234

STOOD UPON, prided herself on, made a fuss about

STORE, 'in store', laid up as in a storehouse

STRAIGHT, immediately

STRANGE, 'Why mak'st thou it so strange?', why do you seem so surprised or shocked?

STRANGERS, foreigners

STRIVE, compete

STRUCK, shot, II i 93

STUDY, thinking, V ii 12

STUPRUM, (Latin) rape

STYX, in Greek mythology, a river at the border of the underworld, which dead souls could not cross until their bodies had been buried

SUBSCRIBE, agree

SUBTLE, treacherous

SUCCESSANTLY, (meaning unclear: following after another? successfully?)

SUCCESSIVE, 'successive title', claim (to the throne) by right of hereditary succession

SUED, pleaded

SUFFER, allow

SUFFRAGES, votes; 'threw the people's suffrages On', cast the people's votes (as their representative) for

SUIT, request

SUNS, 'more suns than one' (the sun was a symbol of kingship)

SUPPOSE, 'vain suppose', empty supposition

SUPPOS'D, (i.e. by Virgil, who told the story in the *Aeneid*), II iii 21

SURANCE, assurance, proof

SURE, undoubtedly, II iv 26, IV ii 72; tightly, V ii 161, 166; harmless, V ii 76; 'make her sure', take care of her, render her harmless; 'make that sure', make sure of that; 'as sure a card . . . set', a person as sure to get her own way as the winning card in a card game ('set')

SURER, 'by the surer side', i.e. by the mother's side (proverbially, motherhood is easier to prove than fatherhood)

SURFEIT ON, eat to excess of

SURPRIS'D, unexpectedly seized; caught, II iii 23

SURPRISED, 'surprised with', suddenly overcome by, II iii 211

SURVEY, 'upon a just survey', after taking a fair view of the case

SUSPICION, 'answer their suspicion', answer for the suspicion they are under

SUST'NANCE, sustenance, food

SUUM CUIQUE, (Latin) 'to each his own'

SWARTH, swarthy, black

SWEET, perfumed, II iv 6

SWELLING, full of passion, V iii 13

SWIFT, swiftly

SYMPATHY, likeness, agreement

TAKE, 'Take this of me', take my word for it; 'take you to', take up; 'take away', clear the table, III ii 81; 'take up', raise (Titus is kneeling), I i 457; 'take up a matter of brawl', settle amicably a case of brawling

TAPER, candle

TARQUIN, (i) Tarquinius Superbus (Tarquin the Proud), the last King of Rome, who was deposed and exiled after his son's rape of Lucrece, and later demanded in vain to return to Rome. (His queen is otherwise unknown, and may be Shakespeare's invention), III i 299; (ii) King Tarquin's son, who raped Lucrece (*see* LUCRECE), IV i 64–5

TARRY, remain

TAURUS, the constellation of the Bull, in the zodiac; 'Taurus' horns' (playing on the cuckold's horns; *see* HORNING)

TAWNY, black

TEDIOUS, laboriously made

TELL, 'Tell on thy mind', Go on, say what you want to say

TEMPER, work upon, IV iv 109; moisten, V ii 200

TENDERS, offers

TEND'RING, consistently with our concern for

TEREUS, *see* PHILOMEL

TERRAS ASTREA RELIQUIT, (Latin) 'Astrea has left the earth' (a quotation from Ovid's *Metamorphoses*, Book I. Astrea, the goddess of justice, abandoned the world at the end of the Golden Age, in disgust at human wickedness)

TESTIMONY, 'for testimony of', to give evidence of

THAT, who, I i 417; that which, I i 408; so that, II iii 237, III i 240; because, IV iv 81; 'that granted', given that fact

THEIR, 'their throats', the throats of those

THEM, (i.e. 'those poor lips'), V iii 171

THEME, *see* HANDLE, III ii 29; *see* PLY, V ii 80

THEREFORE, for that very reason, V ii 164

THERE'S, i.e. there (in the sea) there is, IV iii 9

THINK, 'think you not', aren't you aware, II i 63; 'thinks ... abjectly', thinks me so contemptible

THRACIAN POET, i.e. Orpheus (*see* CERBERUS)

THRACIAN TYRANT, *see* HECUBA

THRASH, thresh

THREAT, threaten

THREW, *see* SUFFRAGES, IV iii 19

THRICE-VALIANT, very valiant

THUS, 'thus much', this much

'TICED, enticed

TIMELESS, untimely

TITAN, the Sun (from the Titan Hyperion, a personification of the Sun)

TO, compared to, V i 90; for, V iii 23

TOFORE, formerly

TOKENS, signs, symbols

TOSSETH, turns over the pages of

TOUCH'D, wounded, IV iv 36

TRAIN'D, lured, V i 104

TRAITORS, treacherous villains, V ii 178

TREASON, (often) betrayal, personal treachery

TRENCHES, furrows, wrinkles

TRIBUNAL PLEBS, (the Clown's blunder for *tribunus plebis*, tribune of the people, *see* TRIBUNES)

TRIBUNES (OF THE PEOPLE), Roman officials who represented the interests of the plebeians, or common people

TRIBUTARY, given as tribute

TRICKS, (i) habits, (ii) trivialities, V i 76

TRIM, 'wash'd ... trimm'd' (as if by a barber); 'trim sport', fine entertainment

TRIUMPHER, one who celebrates a triumph (*see* TRIUMPHS)

TRIUMPHS, (more often 'triumph'), the parade of a victorious Roman general through Rome with his army, spoils and prisoners

TROPHIES, memorials

TROY, the city which fought the Greeks in the ten-year-long Trojan War, and was at last defeated; most of Shakespeare's references relate to the city's capture, sack and burning

TRULL, strumpet

TRUNK, body

TRUST, person whom they trust, I i 181

TULLY'S ORATOR, *De Oratore* ('On the Orator') by the Roman statesman, orator and philosophical writer Marcus Tullius Cicero, a popular book in Shakespeare's time

TURN, 'serve your turns', satisfy you (with a sexual pun: 'turn' often implies sexual intercourse); 'serve the turn', answer the purpose;

'turn me', turn, III i 278; 'turn again', return; 'the turn'd forth', the one who was turned out (of Rome)

TUT, (an impatient exlamation)

TWENTY THOUSAND, *see* MORE, IV ii 44

TYPHON, a monstrous giant, half-serpent, who made war against the gods. (He was not one of the Titans; Shakespeare has his mythology slightly confused)

TYRANNY, ruthless cruelty

UNADVIS'D, unwisely

UNCOUPLE, unleash the hounds

UNCOUTH, (i) unaccustomed, (ii) unknown (i.e. a fear of something unknown)

UNDERTAKE, vouch

UNDONE, ruined

UNFURNISH'D OF, unaccompanied by

UNHALLOWED, unholy, wicked

UNKIND, (i) cruel, (ii) unnatural (lacking in the feelings of 'kind', nature)

UNRECURING, incurable

UNREST, 'for their unrest ... chest', to cause trouble for those who take a charitable donation out of this chest (i.e. who find the gold)

UNSPEAKABLE, inexpressibly great

UP, afoot, II ii 1; 'up and down', entirely, all over

UPRISE, rising

URCHINS, (i) goblins, (or) (ii) hedgehogs (associated with witchcraft)

URGE, force upon our attention, III ii 26

URNS, water-jugs (i.e. his eyes), III i 17

US'D, treated; 'us'd in', treated with

USURP UPON, usurp the rights of (i.e. deprive of their sight)

VAST, (i) enormous, (ii) desolate, waste

VAUNTER, boaster

VENEREAL, of Venus (*see* VENUS)

VENUS, (i) the goddess of love, (ii) the planet Venus, whose influence, in astrology, caused amorousness

VIEW, sight

VILLAIN, servant (with a pun on the modern sense; i.e. Aaron), IV iii 73

VIRGINIUS, a Roman senator who killed his daughter Virginia to save her from being forced to sleep with the corrupt judge Appius Claudius. (This is the common version of the story; Shakespeare, in suggesting that Virginia has already been raped, may be following a different version or simply changing the story to fit Lavinia's situation)

VIRGO, the constellation of the Virgin, in the zodiac

VOUCH, maintain, prove by actions

VULCAN'S BADGE, the horns of a cuckold (Vulcan, the lame smith-god, was married to Venus and cuckolded by Mars)

VULTURE, 'gnawing vulture of', Vulture which gnaws (alluding to the legend of Prometheus)

WAGGON, chariot

WAGGONER, charioteer

WAGS, goes about

WAIT, attend; 'be waited on', be received honourably (ironical)

WALL-EYED, with the iris of the eye discoloured (sometimes used for 'squinting' or 'glaring-eyed' – in any case, a term of abuse)

WAND'RING PRINCE, Aeneas (see DIDO)

WANT, lack

WANTING, lacking

WARDED, protected

WARE, wore

WARRANT, promise, IV iii 112; 'warrants ... courtesy', justifies these words as the sort of courtesy a ruler ought to show

WAS, 'Was ever seen ...', was there ever seen ...?

WASTED, ruined

WATCH'D, stayed awake

WAX, grow, become

WEED(S), clothes

WELKIN, sky

WELL, 'Well ... proportion', you will easily recognise her by (comparing her with) your own appearance

WELL-ADVISED, (i) in his right mind (not 'mad'), (ii) according to an intelligent plan (an ironic double meaning)

WELL-BESEEMING, suitable, fitting

WELL SAID, well done!

WHAT, why, I i 189; that, II i 122; 'what with Aaron', what do you want with Aaron?

WHAT TIME, when

WHEN AS, when

WHEN THAT, when

WHERE, in which, II iv 37

WHEREAT, at which

WHEREFORE, why

WHEREIN, in any way in which, V i 7; in what way, V iii 129

WHEREOF, on which

WHICH WAY, how

WHILES, while; 'whiles that', while

WHO, (i.e. the hand; but the syntax is confused, and this 'who' is left dangling), III ii 9

WHOM, (i.e. Justice), IV iv 24

WILL, (often) want to; which will, II ii 21, 23; 'will I', I will go

WILLING, requesting

WIND (n.), 'have the wind of you', keep a watch on you (as a hunter tracks an animal from downwind of it); (v.) blow, II ii 10 *stage direction*; smell, get wind of, IV i 98

WINK, shut the eyes

WIT, intelligence; 'upon her wit ... wait', i.e. she has the intelligence to command any honour she wants

WITH, (often) by (e.g. II iii 24); 'not with himself', beside himself; 'with all', in all circumstances (?)

WITHAL, as well, I i 278; moreover, IV i 115; with, V i 52

WITNESS, (often) you can tell by (e.g. V ii 22); piece of evidence, II iii 116

WITTY, clever

WOE, 'woe is me', it causes me sorrow

WONT, accustomed

WORD, (i) information, (ii) promise, III i 151; 'Of my word', upon my word

WORKING, carrying out

WORLDLY, of this world

WOT, know

WOULD, wants to; I wish, V iii 173; 'would be sure ... well', wanted to be sure that everything was right

WOUND, *see* SIGHING, III ii 15

WREAK (n.), revenge; 'wreaks', vengeful acts; (v.) avange

WREAKFUL, vengeful

WRIT (n.), writing

WRONG, 'doth me wrong', is unfair to me

WROUGHT, 'so wrought on', had such an effect on

WRUNG WITH, painfully pressed by

YELLOWING, yelling, crying

YESTERNIGHT, last night

YET, even now, III ii 76

YOUNG, i.e. inexperienced, IV i 102

YOUNGLING, kid (contemptuous)

YOUR, 'your womb' (i.e. your mother's womb, which gave you birth)

ZODIAC, the cycle of twelve constellations through which the sun travels in the course of a year

ZOUNDS, (an oath: 'by God's wounds')